LESSONS IN LEADERSHIP:
An Art In The Making

Lessons In Leadership: An Art In The Making

Copyright © 2022 Steven R. Haines

As the author, I have made every effort to ensure that the information in this book was correct at press time. This book is designed to provide encouragement, ideas, values, thoughts, and ideas in the area of personal leadership development. I hereby disclaim any errors, inaccuracies, omissions, or any other inconsistencies herein. Likewise, I do not wish to be party for any loss, damage, or disruption caused by errors or omissions, whether such errors or omissions resulting from negligence, accident, or any other cause. I want all readers to enjoy the book and hope the lessons shared inspire you in your own leadership journey. This publication is meant as a source of valuable information for the reader. Your journey in leadership may yield similar or different experiences that bring about alternative feelings, thoughts, or ideas that I have shared here. Leadership and learning are lifelong journeys worth taking.

All rights reserved. No part of this book may be reproduced or used in any manner without the prior written permission of the copyright owner, except for the use of brief quotations in a book review.

I do want this book to serve as a helpful resource to leaders (especially teachers) so if you have ways that the content can help others then by all means, simply request permissions by reaching out to me: **Advantage-USA@comcast.net**

Paperback: 978-1-7348772-4-3
Ebook: 978-1-7348772-5-0

First paperback edition June 2022

Foreword by Patrick Fitzpatrick
Edited by Patrick Fitzpatrick
Cover art by Lance Buckley Designs
Interior Photographs by Steven R. Haines

Printed by IngramSpark

Steven R. Haines

Foreword

by Patrick Fitzpatrick

My friendship with Steve Haines began in 2010. In the last twelve years we have traveled together to China countless times - our hearts knit together because of our passion for God, our genuine love for the people of China, and our shared vision for what true and effective education should look like. On every trip Steve created unforgettable moments for me and others as he orchestrated speaking engagements and networking events with educational leaders across China. As an alumnus and alumni parent of the private school I lead, Steve has been deeply engaged with the school. He served on my board, coached various sports teams, and even jumped into some middle school history classes as a part time teacher when we were in need. While he invested in our school in these meaningful ways he was also building his summer camp businesses and exploring other entrepreneurial opportunities. I cherish the friendship that we have built through these shared experiences, and from countless personal observations I can tell you that Steve is the real deal - a teacher-leader and a leader of leaders.

I read a lot of books on leadership. I especially appreciate authors who are transparent about their own challenges and failures. I was, and still am, willing to learn vicariously through the mistakes and victories that these leaders openly share. What may have taken these authors years to master is accessible to us if we are willing to be teachable and embrace the principles they share.

Steve Haines's book on leadership offers readers an honest glimpse into life as a leader. When Steve asked me if I would consider editing his manuscript I was flattered. Consequently, I have poured over the truths found within this book. While I would like to think that I may have made some sentence structures sound better, I know already that reading through his book is making me a better leader. Steve gained his wealth of leadership skills through a myriad of adventures that span years and include failures and successes. We have the opportunity to learn these same lessons from the comfort of our favorite recliner while sipping from a mug of coffee (Steve would want this for you).

Devote some time to reading through this book, internalize the lessons contained within, and allow yourself to be transformed into the leader that you are meant to be.

About Patrick Fitzpatrick

Patrick is currently the Head of School at Plumstead Christian School in Bucks County, Pennsylvania where he has served since 2010. He and his beloved wife of thirty-six years enjoy life with five children and two grandchildren. In his free time Patrick enjoys writing children's stories and traveling through China with Steve.

LESSONS IN LEADERSHIP: AN ART IN THE MAKING

Introduction:

The number of leadership-focused, self-help books on the market is staggering. Amazon offers over 57,000 book choices containing the word "leadership" in their title., and with a simple search one can find 'how to' books from notable and distinguished leaders such as John Maxwell, Brandon Burchard, or Tony Robbins. If you are reading this book then you have also managed to discover at least one not-so-notable author with over 30 years of real leadership experience. Congratulations! Maybe we both just get lucky.

I am the amalgamation of all the leaders who have influenced me along the way. My life is an 'art in the making.' Every leader who invested in me, intentionally or unintentionally, has added brushstrokes, patterns, and texture to what is still an unfinished, albeit beautiful, brightly colored canvas. This book is my way of honoring these leaders who contributed to the masterpiece I am becoming.

I also have children and grandchildren with whom I want to share these lessons in leadership I have learned over the years. I hope my

> **YOUR LIFE IS AN ART IN THE MAKING**
>
> *Knowledge is simply good advice waiting to be given, but worthless if you keep it to yourself.*

words inspire them in their journey. Also, my father and father-in-law both left me a legacy of leadership to admire, respect, and humbly try to emulate. I hope in some small way that this book pays homage to their impact on me as well. Finally, I have invested a lot of time and energy training teachers, students, athletes, employees, and summer camp staff, and this book contains elements of lessons I taught to these various groups. I hope these can serve as a resource for leaders.

Someone once told me that ***knowledge is simply good advice waiting to be given, but worthless if you keep it to yourself.*** I have been blessed by good advice my whole life, and I hope this book pays it

Write One Thing You Hope To Learn From Reading This Book

forward as a source of helpful advice I have gleaned from the many lessons in leadership that were poured into me.

Each person is a unique canvas that is being painted as they journey through life. Each painting evolves, always adding color and nuance until one's final breath. Even after our life on earth is over, our influence and our legacy continues as if the masterpiece of our life hangs in a gallery for all to see. Our legacy does not need to begin after we have died. Instead, our legacy can begin right now while we are living and while we are growing. Some view this journey as a slow jog filled with good and bad experiences. These people have the mindset of an endurance runner. They move slowly, and their focus is on covering the distance. They struggle up the hills and try to control their pace downhill. They run in heat, cold, dry, or wet conditions, and they appreciate the beautiful, cool days where the weather makes running effortless. If we embrace the endurance runner's mindset, we will be able to rise above the stress and struggle that shows itself even when we don't want it to.

Consider your moments of great success. How many of these moments were preceded by moments of failure or sorrow? How we view the ups and downs of life and the value we place on these experiences either feeds our fear or feeds our faith.

I love what Carol S. Dweck says in her book, *"Mindset: The Psychology of Success"*

> *The growth mindset allows people to value what they're doing regardless of the outcome. They're tackling problems, charting new courses, working on important issues. Maybe they haven't found the cure for cancer, but the search was deeply meaningful."*

Each person has a myriad of opportunities during his life journey to learn how to absorb, react, grow. We need to value the process as well as the final product. Continually develop a stronger mindset and you will continue to grow. Allow others to add color, pattern, and texture to your life. Be open to their influence and watch your masterpiece take shape.

> *"If parents want to give their children a gift, the best thing they can do is to teach their children to love challenges, be intrigued by mistakes, enjoy effort, and keep on learning. That way, their children don't have to be slaves of praise. They will have a lifelong way to build and repair their own confidence."*
> — Carol S. Dweck

I hope this book encourages you wherever you are in your leadership journey. Along the way, those we lead or follow, those who we mentor or who mentored us, those with whom we spend time all contribute to the painting on what is our life's canvas. Each of us is an emerging piece of art made up by many contributing artists. My goal with this book is to strengthen your leadership skills and help you to develop the endurance runner's mindset so you can thrive through the challenges of life and maximize your leadership influence on others. I am confident that these lessons in leadership will equip you to be a positive influence on those with whom you live and lead. Get ready to paint. There are empty canvases out there who need the beauty and blessing of your leadership.

Steve

Chapter 1: LEADERSHIP IS FOR THE BIRDS

I recall as a young boy talking to my grandmother (at the time she was well into her 80th year of life) about the topic of technology. Looking back now, I regret that I was likely too insensitive or just too plain stupid to appreciate her perspective on the topic. After all, she grew up without a computer, cell phone or even a house phone for most of her days. Aside from being "deprived" of those 'technological advances' she also grew up without the luxury of indoor plumbing. We were talking about the new technology of the internet and her response was that it was "for the birds." She was not impressed with all the internet had to offer, and she was convinced that it would not help her to live, thrive, and enjoy life. Afterall, she had lived without the internet for more than eighty years. She did not see the relevance, and she was not willing to change the way she lived in order to embrace the internet and learn how to operate within it. You know what? Who can blame her! She was right! It was also futile to teach her how to use email. She loved to send and receive regular letters by normal parcel post, and email, to her, was just not the same. She lived a happy and fruitful life until the age of ninety-eight even without the internet and email.

The idiom *"for the birds"* is used to mean that something is useless, meaningless, or worthless. The phrase originated as US Army slang towards the end of WWII. An early example of its use is this piece from *The Lowell Sun*, October 1944, in an interview with a Sergeant Buck Erickson, of Camp Ellis, Illinois: *"Don't take too seriously this belief that we have football at Camp Ellis solely for the entertainment of the personnel - that's strictly for the birds. The army is a winner... the army likes to win - that's the most fortunate thing in the world for America."*

Maybe my grandmother was right. As an octogenarian, she had already learned how to live without the computer or email. It was irrelevant. There was nothing to miss. To her, technology was *"for the birds"* because it did not provide her with any relevant solutions in dealing with her life as a country farm girl.

The topic of leadership, on the other hand, is anything but *"for the birds."* It is relevant for everyone since we all have the opportunity to lead or be led.

Most of my life's work has been in education. I was a classroom teacher for more than 20 years, and throughout my role as teacher, I had the opportunity to influence the lives of my students. Not only was I a classroom teacher, but also served my school as Director of Athletics and as a coach in basketball, soccer, and tennis. As a teacher and coach, I understood my responsibility to help shape the students and athletes who were under my leadership guidance. I took my role seriously, and I tried my best to equip them with skills to meet the demands of their life.

During this same time as a teacher, I also became a business owner when I started my summer camp business. At the time I knew nothing about 'being my own boss' nor did I set out with some entrepreneurial dream. I was hungry to create additional opportunities to survive my low paying private school salary, and I figured the best way to do that was to "stay in my lane" and continue to work with children. I leveraged my love of sports and my experience as a coach to offer sport instruction during the summer. This led to other leadership growth opportunities which allowed me to step out of the full-time classroom and into the role of full-time business owner. What started out as a summer gig to earn extra cash grew into my full-time work. Reflecting back, those early years were formative in shaping my views on how to lead others.

Because life is an ever-evolving journey, my early years of leadership were a testing ground too as I explored tactics and strategies for leading others. Mistakes were made, lessons were learned, lumps were taken, and countless people contributed to helping me succeed along the way. Although I continue to run my summer camp business to this day, I intentionally carve out time to train teachers to effectively embrace their role as leader in the classroom. As I have grown professionally as a trainer of teachers, I have been invited to conduct training seminars in China more than 20 times and to more than 75 cities in this magnificent country. During every trip I have met wonderful people and have been overwhelmed by their hospitality, the amazing food, and such a rich culture and history. The Chinese teachers I have worked with are

> **VALUE YOUR PERSONAL DEVELOPMENT**
>
> **OUR LEVEL OF SUCCESS WILL RARELY EXCEEED OUR LEVEL OF PERSONAL DEVELOPMENT BECAUSE SUCCESS IS SOMETHING WE ATTRACT BY WHO WE BECOME.**
>
> **JIM ROHN**

eager to improve and receptive to change. My message to them applies to every teacher around the globe: teachers are leaders for positive or negative change. Teachers need to embrace the responsibility of the leadership role. In doing so there is value to self and others. Being a teacher leader allows us to influence others, and knowing that this is inherent to the position, teachers need the tools and the mindset to move their students in a positive direction.

I find that many teachers fail to see themselves as leaders. Too many teachers simply see themselves as a giver of knowledge occupied with the mission of teaching students what to think. Sure, they may recognize that students look up to them, but very few seem to consider themselves as leaders who just so happen to be teachers. Do you see the difference? Investing in teachers so that they develop and strengthen their leadership skills is of utmost importance. It is, in fact, the furthest thing from "for the birds." Whether you are a teacher, a business owner, a team leader, or a worker in a business - we all find ourselves in a leadership role with someone to influence. The investment into our own leadership abilities is worth our valuable time because it is relevant to every aspect of who we are and what we do. We need to invest in ourselves, and our sphere of influence beyond ourselves is likely far larger than we realize. Unlike my grandmother who could not see the value of embracing computer technology, I want each reader to see the value, responsibility, and power each of us has to influence others.

While the investment in our leadership is not *"for the birds"* there are some interesting lessons in leadership we can learn *"from the birds."*

Growing up in the northeast United States, Canadian Geese were everywhere. It seemed that every local pond, field, or patch of lush green grass was occupied by a gaggle of geese who were busy feeding and fertilizing it! Instinctively, the Canadian geese migrate south as colder weather arrives. When the cold winds of winter came in, we were always glad to see the flocks heading south in advance of the cold. Interestingly, when the flock flies they take on a very interesting and beautiful "v" shape pattern. I became curious as to why these birds take this pattern "v" shape as opposed to any other shape. Studying the reason why they take this shape provides us with some interesting parallels to help us understand our own leadership journey.

Ask a group of people to explain what a leader is, and you might get some typical responses. One common view is that the leader is the one out in front, leading the group. The image of the leader is one who speaks in front of the company or team, the one who makes a keynote or state of the union speech, or the one who is the voice or face of the company. The term "leader" is given to the visible spokesperson in charge, a.k.a. the boss. But effective leadership is not always reserved for the voice and the face because many leaders realize their leadership comes from being part of the team that makes things happen. As I studied the behavior of the Canadian geese, I began to see them as a symbol to better understand how a leader is also part of the team they lead. It is why the term teamwork is such an important concept for any leader to grasp.

Two parallel lessons we can learn from the Canadian geese. First, when the flock departs, one bird takes the point position in the "v" formation. Clearly the lead bird who is the perceived and visible leader flying out in front sets the direction of flight for those following behind. Not surprisingly, the lead bird expends considerably more energy than the others in the formation. The leader is breaking the headwind, bearing the responsibility to guide the group in the direction of their destination. The energy it takes to fly point is more than the energy spent by others in the formation. We see the truth of this concept in racing where the lead runner, driver, or cyclist creates a draft for those immediately behind them. Those in the lead are closer to the finish line, but it comes at a cost of fuel and energy consumption at a greater rate than those benefiting from the leader's draft. Unlike in a race where there is only one winner, the geese are not in a race to the destination. As a result, the lead bird only takes that point position for a short period. Their innate sense of teamwork within the flock kicks in and suddenly the flock rearranges its pattern. A new leader emerges, and a new draft is created. The lead bird knows the importance of sharing the responsibility. She is willing to fly in front, but she also recognizes her need to yield the lead position and fall back in formation as a member of the overall team and for the good of the overall team.

Secondly, the flying formation shape ("V") presents a picture of protection and safety as they fly together. To predators, flying in the V-formation makes the individuals in the flock appear as one large object (think Stealth bomber) flying in the sky. To their enemies, they appear as one large object, not a collection of individual birds. The illusion of size casts fear in predators who stay clear of this much larger opponent. The unity found in the formation deters predators, and in that same way effective teamwork and unity within an organization can provide safety and security for the group. This is where the saying, "teamwork makes the dream work" makes sense.

Because I have focused most of my leadership training for teachers, I would like to direct some thoughts specifically to them. If you are not a teacher, I believe that you will find these lessons applicable to you as well.

Let's first look at the role of teacher

Teachers are hired to communicate data, teach processes, theories, practices, and critical thinking skills. All of this is meant to better help students learn how to think. As I mentioned earlier, I spend a great deal of time convincing teachers that they are in fact leaders who happen to be teachers. My goal is to empower them to spend time and energy sharpening their leadership skills which will, in turn, enhance their effectiveness as a communicator, teacher, and facilitator. I have met so many teachers who have never considered themselves to be a leader. They see themselves first as a giver of information to be learned, regurgitated, and then assessed. Being a teacher-leader is so much more than this!

Now, let's look at the role of student

In countless situations, I have observed many teachers, principals, and parents, who treat students primarily as brain sponges who absorb the knowledge fed so they can be assessed, graded, then ranked. Keep in mind the assessment, grades, and ranking are compared to others in the class or grade. These "grades" transfer as an indication of their IQ aptitude and class ranking status. Suddenly, students who have been told by others that "each student is a unique individual who learns differently and should therefore be celebrated" are now thrown into the same pot of soup and cooked over the stove of comparison as if each student was the exact same ingredient adding to the singular flavor of the entire soup. What happened to diversity of the learner or learning style? What happened to differentiated instruction when so many assessments lack similar focus to variety? We know that not all students are the same. Teachers are called to lead students with diverse learning styles, emotional strengths, and weaknesses, learning differences, and social challenges. For teacher leaders to be seen as just the giver of knowledge diminishes their role and their overall importance and influence on those they lead. For the school, principal, and teacher who embraces this version of the role as leader this suddenly breaks open a new horizon of influence and outreach. The teacher leader recognizes the diversity presented by each learner and they search for the best way to grow the group as well as each individual student. This new approach unleashes the power to influence each student's EQ (emotional intelligence) not just their IQ.

An effective teacher leader creates a culture of unity in what can appropriately be considered the classroom's flying formation. Yes, the teacher leader may fly in front to absorb the headwind and guide the class towards the target destination, but a great teacher also knows when to drop back into formation and let the student(s) take the lead. Doing so allows the teacher to focus on the 'class culture,' ensuring that it is a place where curiosity is celebrated, where risks can be taken safely, and where mistakes can be handled with grace and treated as an opportunity for growth and learning. This does not diminish the teacher's authority. Instead, this approach promotes the idea that learning can be a team effort. As students take the lead, the teacher can better celebrate each child's uniqueness as he or she manages the emotional safety of the learning space by giving greater attention to learning styles while building strategies for community and collaboration. Good teacher leaders do not always fly in front. They know when to provide their class with the benefit of draft, but they also know that asking students to take the lead grows them in amazing ways.

Regardless of what you or I may think of the late Apple CEO Steve Jobs, including his noted successes and failures, I find in his story an interesting lesson on the importance of teamwork and unity. In 1986, shortly after he was forced out of Apple, Jobs purchased a small computer manufacturing company by the name of Pixar. Pixar has gone on to produce some of the most amazing and successful animated movies of all time. Pixar movies have been consistently among the highest revenue grossing productions released. After outgrowing a previous facility, Jobs chose a large, abandoned three building warehouse to serve as their new home. His hired architects presented him with renovation and redesign plans that kept the three buildings separated but carved up into individual offices where computer scientists, animators, and executives could find quiet workspaces. When Jobs reviewed the plans he said, "absolutely not!" He emphatically wanted one large space with an atrium room that would serve as the hub and central connector to all three buildings. His vision was for one unified space where creators could gather, share, and collaborate. Confused, the architects asked Job what he saw as the most important function of Pixar? Jobs replied, "it's the interaction of our employees." Jobs wanted the space to foster unity of sharing, creating, and collaboration rather than isolation. This was his way of flying Pixar in the V-formation.

Jobs knew that for Pixar to be successful, creators needed to collaborate. He wanted creativity to flow and for the energy produced from such creativity to be shared. He also knew that the physical space could foster or impede this process. In this way he brought together a diversity of talents, personalities, and styles to form a strong, unified, and creative staff. Maybe Jobs was choosing the V-formation because he knew that from time to time the point person would change as the need arose. He believed that the unity of the Pixar team was greater than the sum of all individual creators working in isolated offices. Jobs understood that when people gather for a clear and supported purpose great things can happen. When the team culture is nourished in this way, creativity, curiosity, and collaboration blossom. Not surprisingly, so does the social and emotional health of the team members.

For the past few years, the COVID-19 pandemic has forced us to not gather but to isolate. I won't get into the definition of "forced," but we were told to isolate for the protection of self and others. What was initially promoted to be thirty days to "slow the spread" or "flatten the curve" turned into a life-transforming shift from team to individual isolation. Many moved to remote learning or working from home, and our idea of collaboration was reduced to a one-dimensional image of co-workers on a computer screen in Teams or Zoom. Consequently, new emerging research is revealing an increase in emotional and stress related issues (alcoholism, depression, suicide) arising from the oxymoron term 'social distancing.' There is no social benefit when distancing from others. Many workers, students and teachers miss the energy of community with others around the lunch table, break room, basketball court, playground, or courtyard. When people gather they talk, share, listen, laugh, cry, and play together. Humans are wired to connect to other humans. Human connection is necessary for healthy social and emotional developmental needs to take place.

I want to leave you with 3 reminders that I hope strengthen your leadership development.

1. **REMEMBER THAT NOT ALL LEADERS ARE APPOINTED OR ELECTED.** To lead is to influence. This is the simplest and most effective definition of leadership. Whether you teach students, manage others, or are part of a larger team flying somewhere in the V-formation, you have the opportunity to influence others from any flight position. Embrace this responsibility, celebrate the opportunity, and boldly believe in your ability to influence others in a positive way.

2. **LEAD IN UNITY, NOT IN ISOLATION.** Remember Pixar's atrium building designed as a unifying, collaborative space where ideas are shared and exchanged. Out of collaborative interaction ideas are born, tested, modified, and further inspired because of the energy generated from interaction with others. Be a leader who places high value in team unity and develop a culture and the physical spaces that facilitate collaboration. .

3. **WHEN YOU LEAD, FLY IN A BOLD AND CLEAR FORMATION LIKE THE CANADIAN GEESE.** Work with others so each member can benefit from the draft created by the leader currently flying up front. There is strength in the formation. It is easy to follow the lead bird, and the formation itself provides greater defense from predators.

> **Your Personal Reading Takeaway**

Learning to be a leader is definitely NOT "for the birds," but we can learn leadership lessons from them. Leaders work together in unity with others. When it is your turn, take the lead position in the formation and provide draft for those with whom you work. Don't be afraid to fly in the back of the formation for a while as you carefully observe those ahead of you. Watch, learn, and benefit from the draft they create. Leadership growth is a slow and steady process of personal and professional development, and it requires you to have a strong mindset and perseverance. People need leaders, and people are especially quick to follow someone when they sense that he or she is sincere and caring. The first step in the growth process is embracing your role as leader. Leaders always have the opportunity to influence others, and quite often you don't even realize the impact you are having. By accepting your role as leader, regardless of your title or position, you embrace the responsibility that comes as an influencer of others. When ready, and when appropriate, you will slip into the lead position. When you do, remain a vital part of the team you lead. Good luck as you build your personal leadership characteristics.

Knowledge is simply good advice waiting to be given, but it is worthless if you decide to keep it to yourself.

Chapter 2 DIRTY LENSES SEE THINGS DIFFERENTLY

As I walked into the optometrist's office I was guided to sit behind a crazy, futuristic looking machine. When the optometrist sat facing me, he asked me to press my face up against the phoropter, the binocular-looking contraption. Positioning his face just inches away from mine, he began looking inside of my eyes. The next step in the exam was reading the dreaded letter chart on the wall. After positioning myself behind the red line taped onto the floor, he asked me to cover one eye with what looked like a plastic serving spoon. Hanging on the wall twenty feet away was a letter chart I was expected to read. Nervously, I began calling out the letters. I began boldly but gradually began to lose confidence as the size of the letters began shrinking. Surprisingly, but also proudly, the doctor awarded me a good report with near perfect vision. My eyes were good, and he assured me that I could continue to see the beauty of the world around me.

No matter what we look at, good vision is essential so that we see things clearly and accurately. Even though I was granted a clear vision report from the optometrist, if I proceeded to leave and put on a pair of sunglasses with dirty lenses my clear vision report would be meaningless because I would not be seeing anything clearly. Dirty lenses obscure the clear and accurate perspective. They distort what we really see. We all recognize the importance of seeing things clearly. Those who wear glasses need to clean their lenses when they get dirty. Those who wear contacts wear them to improve the clarity of their vision. To see things clearly, we must have clear lenses.

The great American inventor, Thomas Alva Edison (1847-1931) has contributed to 1,093 patents for his inventions. His early phonograph invention created a way for people to listen to and enjoy recorded music. He is also credited with perfecting the incandescent light bulb which forever changed the way we light up our homes and businesses. His ingenious inventions are significant but driving this creative and clever mind was a man with a remarkable ability to view things with a clear and accurate perspective that was unmatched by most.

On December 10, 1914, at age 67, the building that served as the base of business and an incubator for ongoing inventions caught fire. As the fire ravaged and consumed the factory with many of their past, present, and future products and inventions, Edison and his twenty-four-year-old son Charles stood by helplessly and watched years of collective work being consumed and destroyed by the unforgiving force of fire. The next morning, with the smoke still rising from the ashes, Edison and Charles once again stood in disbelief at the rubble of smoldering ruins. Who could blame him for being heartbroken or even angry at the overwhelming loss? Despite their utter loss, Edison told Charles, *"There is great value in disaster. All of our mistakes are burned up. Thank God we can start anew."*

These are some of the most meaningful words Edison shared with his son - inspirational words that demonstrated to Charles and to me Edison's remarkable leadership ability to see things differently. His lenses were not dirty! Edison chose to view the calamity with a clarity that only the strongest of leaders can see. Where others simply saw the destruction of his work and ideas, he was able to see the fire as an opportunity to erase previous mistakes and start anew. He chose to see things differently.

per·spec·tive-*a particular attitude toward, or way of regarding something; a point of view.*

Seeing an object clearly is essential to establish perspective related to height/width, depth, shape, and distance of what is being viewed. Clear perspective is critical when driving an automobile. Without it an accident may happen when, for example, one driver who is turning misjudges the distance or speed of an approaching vehicle. A basketball player needs an accurate perspective while shooting to have a decent chance of making a basket. A quarterback needs depth perspective to hit a target moving towards or away from him. Likewise, a racecar driver moving at the heart-racing speed of 190 mph needs a clear perspective to safely maneuver around the other 25 racers jammed on the small racetrack. A clear perspective is not only essential for athletic success, it may also be the difference between life and death. Leadership does not always deal with life and death situations, but effective leadership requires proper perspective.

How is it that two people can look at the same image yet not have the same perspective? Below is the famous image that first appeared on an 1888 German postcard, later adapted by British cartoonist, William Ely Hill, for inclusion in a 1915 humor magazine with the title, "My Wife and My Mother-in-Law." Stephen Covey (and others) used this image to illustrate how we may all view the same image differently. If you never have before, look and decide for yourself whether you see an old or young woman?

Whether you see the old woman or the young woman may involve the deeper analytical study of object perception. My purpose in using this illustration is to simply state that many times leaders must realize that even though something may seem obvious to us, others may see the same thing but from a different perspective. Accepting the fact that we all see things differently can help leaders better adjust perceptions and expectations. It is also a striking reminder that we need greater empathy and understanding for those who have different viewpoints.

We all face great challenges and struggles in life when we feel like Edison and Charles watching the destruction of our work and dreams. Every leader faces times of challenge, but we also face far more times where seemingly simple situations require us to carefully consider how our perspective may differ from others. Effective leadership requires proper perspective. We may be looking at the same image or circumstance that others are looking at, and we need to remember that we may not be viewing it in the same way. We must remember that although our perception is our reality, it may not be the same reality for those we lead. Our lens of experience impacts our perspective, and

> **IMPORTANCE OF A CLEAR AND ARTICULATED VISION**
>
> **THE VERY ESSENCE OF LEADERSHIP IS THAT YOU HAVE TO HAVE A VISION. IT'S GOT TO BE A VISION YOU ARTICULATE CLEARLY AND FORCEFULLY ON EVERY OCCASION. YOU CAN'T BLOW AN UNCERTAIN TRUMPET.**
>
> REVEREND THEODORE HESBURGH

since we all look through a different lens of experience, we often interpret what we see differently. These differences can cause rifts, factions, conflicts or even dismantle our influence as a leader if we are not careful and sensitive to recognize them.

As I shared in the previous chapter, my simple definition of leadership is influence. Our ability to see things differently will expand our influence and ability to lead. Because leaders cast a vision and must communicate well with others, we must be sensitive to the different perspectives of others. Understanding this helps us to manage and diffuse the conflicts that may arise. It is also important that when leaders see things differently, we take the time to appreciate the perspectives of others.

In 1911, the unsinkable Titanic was launched on its maiden trans-Atlantic voyage. The Titanic was the biggest, best, and strongest ship ever built. Sadly, it could not live up to the hype as it struck an iceberg that tore through its steel and sent more than 1,500 people to their horrific death. Had the iceberg been clearly seen, they would have steered clear of it. The thing to remember about any iceberg is that very little of it is visible above the waterline. Most of the iceberg is out of sight beneath the waterline. Leaders are expected to have the vision and foresight to not only see the obvious obstacles but also the wisdom and experience to see what lies beneath. Situations we are called to lead through are often far more dangerous than what is clearly visible. HOW you see something affects WHAT you see.

To see things differently leaders, need determination and ability to manage our perspective. What we see may be different from what others see. If all we do is force our perspective on others without considering the perspective of others, we position ourselves in a place of expected conflict. Leaders need to arm themselves with the proper lens of positive attitude and consideration for others. Stand in the shoes of Thomas Edison and his son Charles. Gaze upon the ashes of what were once their dreams and realities, and then muster the

strength and hope to recognize the "great value in disaster." Where most people see only destruction and loss, Edison saw things differently. Yes, the fire consumed his hard work, inventions, and ideas, but it also provided hope through the cleansing of all his previous mistakes. Where most would see ashes, Edison had a different perspective - one full of optimism for a fresh and clean slate to start again.

I offer three tips for how we may learn to see things differently:

1. **SEE WITH YOUR EYES BUT CHECK THE CLARITY OF YOUR LENS.** For those who wear glasses I am sure you can relate. Having glasses is great but useless if the lenses are so dirty one cannot see clearly. Just as one would not want to view a planet through a dirty telescope lens, we must make sure our lens of perspective is not dirty. Consider the views and perspectives of others. Do not just focus on the disaster but the hope that can be found in the ashes. Your lens of leadership is shaped by your experience and the attitude you choose. To see things differently, check the clarity of your lens to ensure you are seeing and considering the perspective of others.

2. **SEE WITH YOUR EARS.** The Greek philosopher Epictetus is credited with giving some brilliant advice: *"you have two ears and one mouth, so listen twice as much as you speak."* Leaders do not have to be the loudest in the room. Volume of voice does not always bring the desired results to get people to listen. Leaders should always listen more than they speak, and when they do speak, they should carefully choose their words with the highest degree of caution. We can learn far more from listening than from talking.

3. **SEEK ANOTHER VIEWPOINT** When faced with a challenge, ask your trusted advisors and friends for their perspective. You may find you see things differently, and different perspectives have value. Maybe you see the old woman in the picture, but they see the young woman. Why? We all see things differently. Maybe you see the iceberg from an "above the waterline" perspective, but your friends may see something much larger lying beneath.

Just because we see things differently from others does not always make one perspective right and the other wrong. It is not always that simple. Because our perspective lenses are shaped by different experiences a great leader is willing to see the situation from the viewpoints and perspectives of others. As leaders desire greater influence, our intent should always be to make the best decision possible after considering the perspectives of others. Sometimes the opinions shared are clear validation of our own perspective, and other times they are cautious and contrary perspectives. Strive to see things differently. Conduct a careful search for a full and clear perspective and watch your influence as a leader grow.

> **Hope or Ashes?**
>
> **IS YOUR LEADERSHIP PERSPECTIVE STRONG ENOUGH TO SEE THE HOPE WITHIN THE ASHES?**
>
> **WRITE YOUR TAKEAWAY THOUGHTS?**

Knowledge is simply good advice waiting to be given, but it is worthless if you decide to keep it to yourself.

Chapter 3 THE POWER OF POSITIVE MESSAGES

Can you recall the last time you received positive feedback from your boss or supervisor? Have you ever received praise from a colleague for the great work you have done? When was the last time someone told you how amazing you were? We all love to receive positive messages of praise and affirmation. When we hear praise, it makes us feel great, and it is usually something we can remember and recall for quite a while. Research recognizes the power words can have. Words of praise can elevate our self-esteem and make our spirits soar. Equally, words of criticism can leave us heartbroken and easily send our spirits into a spiral of sadness. There are many sayings about the power of words, and one I find memorable is, "words don't kill, but they sure can destroy."

If we are honest, we have all been on the receiving and giving end of both positive and painful words. To this day I still cringe at the memory of negative or hurtful words I knowingly and unknowingly may have said to others in middle school, high school, or college. Why did I even open my big mouth in the first place! I was always told, "if you don't have something nice to say then don't say anything at all." This was advice I clearly should have lived by but didn't! I hope it was not my intention to say words that hurt, but I think many times the words we say cut deeply into the hearts of others. This is reason enough to guard our tongue with greater caution and restriction.

I wrote about Thomas Edison in the previous chapter. There is another wonderful story about Thomas Edison as a young child that might help drive home the point I am trying to make about the power of positive messages. One day, Thomas Edison came home from school, and upon entering the house he handed his mother a note from his teacher. Not knowing, but nonetheless afraid of the contents of this note, Edison hesitantly delivered the note then quickly tried to disappear to escape what he was sure would be impending punishment for bad behavior or poor performance at school. Before he could move, his mother opened the note and read it silently to herself. The young boy now frozen with fear looked carefully at her face trying to determine whether this was a good or bad note. Suddenly, her eyes began to fill with tears. "What does it say, mother?" Edison asked with concern in his voice. Through the tears his mother spoke these words, "your son is a genius. This school is too small for him and doesn't have enough good teachers to train him. Please teach him yourself." Never before was the young boy so proud of the praise offered by his teacher. His mother embraced her son, assured him he was special and that, as per the teacher's request, he would no longer attend that school. Her words, spoken through the tears, became magical words that boosted the young boy's self-confidence and inspired his insatiable curiosity that undoubtedly contributed to the upward trajectory of his life. He grew to become the most significant inventor in over 100 years of American history.

A number of years after Edison's mother passed away, he was looking through some old family photos when he came across a folded piece of paper tucked in the back corner of the drawer that served as his mother's work desk. Curious as always, he opened it and read the actual words written by his teacher all those years earlier. "Your son is mentally ill. We won't let him come to school anymore." Sitting alone, Edison wept for hours before writing these words into his diary, "Thomas Alva Edison was a mentally ill child that, by a hero mother, became a genius of the century." The power of positive messages given by his "hero mother" helped change the trajectory of his young boy's life. Words that could easily have been devastating were instead altered to inspire an even deeper curiosity and self-confidence. As leaders, parents, husbands, wives, girlfriends, boyfriends or just friends, the power of positive messages can change someone's life, and they might also help change history.

We have an old American saying, "sticks and stones may break my bones, but words can never hurt me." Quite frankly, I disagree with that saying. Words may not break bones, but they can either crush or elevate someone's spirit. The more appropriate rephrase should be, "sticks and stones may break my bones, but words can definitely change my brain." That is right! Words can literally change our brain. "Scientific studies actually show that positive and negative words not only affect us on a deep psychological level, but they have a significant impact on the outcome of our lives." *(see endnotes for a very good read)

> **REMEMBER THE POWER OF YOUR WORDS**
>
> **BE CAREFUL WITH WORDS. ONCE THEY ARE SAID THEY CAN ONLY BE FORGIVEN, NOT FORGOTTEN.**
>
> UNKNOWN

In Words Can Change Your Brain, authors Andrew Newberg, M.D. and Mark Robert Waldman reveal, "a single word has the power to influence the expression of genes that regulate physical and emotional stress." Positive words such as peace and love can alter the expression of genes, strengthening those key areas in our brain called the frontal lobes that promote the brain's motivational centers. Literally speaking, positive words generate greater motivation for the recipient. As powerful as positive words are, the reverse effect can also be true of negative language. Negative messages disrupt specific genes that play a key role in protecting us from stress. Humans are hardwired to worry. Our brain can sense a threat to our survival, and this, in turn, flips a switch in our central nervous system, causing the sympathetic nervous system to turn on. . When the sympathetic nervous system is engaged we enter a fight or flight response. This happens when we perceive a threat. Just like positive words promote curiosity, negative words promote stress.

Research reveals that even ONE single negative word can increase the activity in the part of the brain (amygdala) responsible for our fear. Even one negative word can cause your brain to release dozens of stress-producing hormones and neurotransmitters that interrupt the healthy function of our brain. Angry words send alarm messages racing through the brain, causing a partial and protective shutdown to our ability to process rational thinking. Have you ever watched a scary movie? When someone is frightened and the sympathetic nervous system (the fight or flight system) turns on, normal brain function is interrupted. This system impedes one's basic ability to coordinate movements or make calculated decisions.

Additionally, research also discovered that the longer we concentrate on positive words the more we begin to affect, train, or exercise areas of the brain that produce good neurotransmitters associated with our mental and emotional health. This is significant because if we can focus on positive thoughts and positive messages from external sources we can build a protective defense against stress-inducing hormones. This is one exercise routine I love because it does not require me to go to the gym and sweat. Plus, membership inside my brain is free.

Thomas Edison's mother handled the note brilliantly. Had she simply read the exact words written by the teacher, the damage to Edison's curiosity, self-confidence, and motivation may have altered the course of history. Instead, the positive words translated by his hero mother encouraged him to continue to think in a bold, positive, and self-confident way. These positive words may have set him on a life-course that the original negative words would have derailed. At the end of his life, Edison was famously quoted as saying, "My mother was the making of me. She was so true, so sure of me, and I felt I had someone to live for, someone I must not disappoint." The hero of a mother understood the power of positive messages and helped feed one of the greatest minds in human history. Guarding our words is one of the great challenges in leadership.

Just like we need to train our body to be healthy, our brains require the same commitment to exercise in order to maintain our mental health. We can positively train our brain and without a monthly membership or physical exertion. Consider these three brain training exercises and how you might use them for yourself or for the benefit of those you lead.

Think positively about yourself. Write down five positive things you love about your core characteristics, which includes your personality, character, morals, feelings, etc. This is the first step in training our minds to focus on personal positive thinking. Avoid focusing on the list of physical attributes, vocational skills or talents that you may also love about yourself.

Live with Intentional Positivity. Find a quiet place without distraction. Set a timer for four minutes. Sit comfortably and meditate on the five positive words or messages that you wrote down in step one. Then, speak the positive words or phrases and mentally focus on what these words or phrases mean and how believing in them can affect how you act and live. Make a commitment to repeat these words or phrases throughout the day as you train your brain in the power of positive messages.

Spread The Positivity. Having a positive self-image will manifest itself, helping us to see the positive things in others. Now that you have identified and concentrated on your personal positive messages, select someone you want to edify by sharing the power of positive messages with them. Don't make this about you. Be the hero-friend who builds them up with positive messages about what they mean to you and the positive ways in which they influence you. Watch how spreading positivity changes their day and maybe the history of your connection with them.

Students hear negative messages every day. Messages that they are not good enough, not smart enough, not pretty enough, not skinny enough, or not stylish enough when compared to their peers. ATELOPHOBIA is the fear of imperfection; of not being enough. Instead of feeling contentment, satisfaction, or hopeful, the pervasive message is negative - that one does not meet the "standard." Many students do not feel smart, confident, or successful in the classroom because they use their earned grade or score as the key factor to determine how smart they are. Likewise, the educational system (teachers, parents, report cards) use the earned grades to quantify how much knowledge has been learned and how students compare with each other. This cycle creates stress in students. When stress is elevated, our ability to think, move, act and react clearly is inhibited. Many teachers have unknowingly created a classroom atmosphere of extreme stress for many students. Because we have learned from research that each positive message impacts the brain and reduces stress, we also know that when negative messages dominate, the fear of imperfection breeds the consequence of a negatively skewed perception of reality.

Think about those whom you teach, lead, and influence. What you say can change the trajectory of their lives. Leaders influence others by what they do and by what they say. I can easily identify with Thomas Edison because I too had a teacher that had a life-changing impact on me. Fortunately, my hero teacher did not say I was stupid or mentally ill when I was not performing up to either he academic standards or my true potential. Instead, through his positive messages, he did help me see a true picture of my core characteristics. He didn't stop here either. He then pushed me to exercise my leadership skills, changing the trajectory of my life. Instead of feeling like I was not 'good enough,' he helped me understand that my expressed desire to 'be better' required more effort than I was consistently giving at that time. He believed in my potential to lead, he reinforced his belief in me with trust and opportunity, and he backed it all up with the power of positive messages.

The young Thomas Edison would go on and prove to be anything but "mentally ill." With over 1,000 patents to his credit, I wonder if his teacher ever regretted writing those words to his mother. I hope so! Had his mother read the exact words as they had been written, what impact may that have had on one of the most curious and creative minds of the century? Instead, because of the deep love of a hero mother for her son, she lovingly delivered words to brain-train her son with the life-changing power of positive messages. Teachers have many opportunities to make or break the confidence of a student. Leaders have many occasions to 'make or break' the will and the heart of those they lead. Parents possess the power to make or break the spirit and will of their child. Carefully considered and chosen words should be delivered with love and thoughtfulness. When we speak out of frustration, we often render the true message meaningless. Matthew 12:36 reads," I tell you, on the day of judgment people will give account for every careless word they speak."(ESV)

Knowledge is simply good advice waiting to be given, but worthless if you keep it to yourself.

Try this simple exercise to help build your positive personal message.

Complete the statement:

One characteristic I love most about myself is:

_____

The one person who can easily make me smile:
_____

I feel best about myself when I:
_____

I am most proud of myself because I:
_____

The person who inspires me most is:
_____

One characteristic that other people admire about me is:
_____

Today I will share a positive message with:
_____

Learn how to use the power of positive messages in leadership

Learning how to guide others while leading takes a lifetime of learning. Young leaders tend to struggle with the balance between the desire to be respected and the desire to be liked. It is true that almost every leader wants to be liked AND respected. Some leaders feel that if they give too much praise or positive words to those they lead then they will not be able to be firm or direct when the time comes. At the same time, how can I lead others and have them like me?

On the other side of the spectrum is the cranky career leader who is beyond jaded and worn out with "people" and comes across as angry, intolerant, and impersonal. These leaders seem to care nothing about being liked and simply want to maintain the distance between

WRITE A POSTIVE MESSAGE TO YOURSELF

leadership and the worker. This keeps them in the position of control. In their misguided perspective, control is leadership.

Every leader should appreciate the individuals they lead. Every individual has a story, dreams, desires, goals, strengths, and weaknesses; all elements to be respected. I believe the leader who invests time and attention in getting to know as many of those individual's "stories" as they can is in a much better position to influence. I find that when I know a person's story I am better equipped to offer positive messages that will be more genuine and meaningful. Knowing more about the person simply deepens my understanding of them and how I can more effectively lead.

Build a culture of positive messages Here are some suggestions:

Begin by subtly posting positive messages throughout the workplace.

Add a short positive message or quote on your email signature.

Send a handwritten note to those you want to encourage with a positive message.

Share your goal to build a more positive culture with managers who may have more contact with a greater number of workers than you do.

Surprise someone with a cup of coffee and a short-handwritten note.

Chapter 4: THE MAIN THING

We all lead busy lives. Rarely do you encounter someone who does not say how busy they are at work, and that they have little time to enjoy the fun things of life. It seems as if we manage to fill every spare moment with other essential (or non-essential but demanding) "things." Managing our schedule of time demands, balancing our perceived priorities, and doing it all with a level of sanity seems increasingly more difficult. Those able to achieve the elusive balance seem to walk and live with a level of harmony desirable to most. The delicate balancing act is not just for those still actively in the workforce. I hear the same lament from those who are retired and are supposed to have all the time in the world. Time is precious, and it is something we chase to control.

Like most, I too have things in life that tug on my time demands. At times I feel I cannot add one more thing to my already overflowing plate of responsibilities. I am married with five children and a grandparent to four beautiful grandchildren. I manage multiple businesses incubated from scratch, and I give attention to personal and business investments that all require some level of involvement. I can easily find myself wishing I had more time. I find each demand on time an important and worthy use of my effort, energy, and attention. Each demand is deemed necessary and worthwhile, and each provides me with happiness and satisfaction. Even so, they all contribute to stress and anxiety levels that need to be managed.

How do we keep the main thing the main thing?

In my teacher training funshops, as I prefer to call them, I like to use a visual prop to illustrate the busyness of life we are all trying to balance/manage. Using a jar labeled as the "life jar" I drop 8-10 golf balls inside the jar. Each golf ball is labeled using words like health, food, water, shelter, friends, career, and money. I top it off with

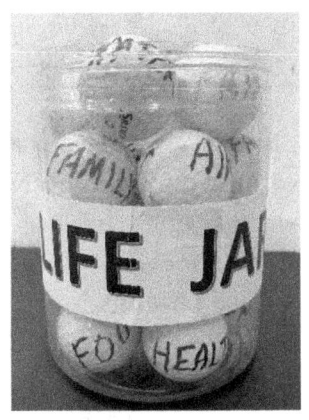
Life Jar

multiple family balls for the various pulls from immediate and extended family. Each ball deposited inside the life jar represents a major life need that is a significant demand on our time and attention. These are considered major things that we want and need but that also must be balanced. With little effort, all the balls fit inside, and the life jar visually appears full.

If I stopped the illustration there, we could all find the ability to manage life. But most of us want more out of life than just these big things. I now take some small pebbles, and as I pour them over the golf balls, I announce that these pebbles represent the many other important things that contribute to a rich and full life. These pebbles represent things like our career promotions, second jobs, homes, money and investments, social life, etc. These may not be the 'biggest' things in life, but they often pull significantly on our energy,

contribute to our worry, and present a real challenge to our life balance. With the smaller pebbles now in the jar, it appears completely full. Pebbles surround and fill what used to be open spaces between the golf balls. As I hold up the life jar I say, "our life jar now appears full, doesn't it?" The answers are always unanimous.

Important Life Things

But, up to this point, most of what we added into the life jar all seem necessary and desirable things that often feel like the bare minimum. I mean, would I really cut out spending time with family, my children, or my career? Can any of these priorities really be removed from the time demand inside my life jar? Of course not. As with all other items currently in the jar, family is essential. With that I introduce the next factor in balancing our life jar demands represented by the tiny grains of sugar. As I slowly begin to pour sugar into the life jar it serves to illustrate the UN-demands in life like the "unexpected, unforeseen, and usually unwanted" things we are all forced to spend time doing in life. Sadly, we now add a global pandemic to the list of unexpected, unforeseen, and certainly unwanted things in our lives. Unwanted things like sickness, job loss, career change, family emergency, loss of loved ones, or even a global pandemic weigh on us and demand our time. These new challenges represented by sugar may not be wanted, but they are now forced to be added to the already full life jar. As we seek to find more capacity inside the life jar we experience stress, depression, anxiety, worry and, of course, additional demand on our evaporating time and energy capacity. The demand on our time and energy increases along with our stress and anxiety. With a little shake of the jar, the sugar finds its way in and around the golf balls, filling in all the nooks and crannies. Almost magically, additional space appears. I proceed to add even more sugar until it is filled to the brim. As I glance at the participants, I can see they easily identify with the UN-demands they experience in life. "Is there any more space in our life jar?" A resounding "NO" is emphatically shouted from the audience.

The "UN" demands in life

We know that if our life were filled with nothing but UN-demands, we would rarely smile or find a consistent source of joy and happiness. Life may have UN-demands, but hopefully our life is filled with far more times of pleasure than pain. We must protect some time for moments of joy. We need to find space inside our life jar to ensure that we have experiences that bring happiness. But how do we add these moments to a jar that is already filled to the brim? Is it even possible? The visibly full jar reveals the obvious answer: no! I then hold up a cup of hot tea to represent the pleasurable moments we all seek and must have to bring pure joy and love to our busy lives.

In a moment of confession, I reveal that one of my great pleasures in life is sitting in a quiet or quaint setting (preferably a Starbucks or wine bar) with my wife, child, or close friend to simply enjoy the quiet time to share and connect with meaningful people in my life. As I pour the hot tea into the life jar I remind them that although life seems too full, these are special and important moments that will intentionally add happiness to our life. These simple times can refresh and re-energize our souls, no matter how busy life may appear. To enjoy these refreshing moments, we must intentionally add them, and to do so requires that we find another gear of capacity. These moments of slight rejuvenation require us to find another internal gear into which we must shift. I call this extra, overdrive gear GRIT. The word GRIT is an acronym that stands for GUTS, RESILIENCE, INITIATIVE, and TENACITY.

As I hold up the life jar that is visibly filled with all the nooks and crannies packed solid with the UN-demands packed tightly around the other more important things inside our life jar it is as if the room is looking for a ray of hope, rescue, and salvation. I now hold up a hot cup of tea representing special rejuvenating and refreshing moments. Intentionally and slowly pouring the tea into the life jar immediately melts away the sugar, exposing new additional space among the golf balls and pebbles. I glance at the faces to see their frowns turn to smiles. I announce that each of us possesses the unique ability to learn, adapt, endure, grow, and morph into an even better version of ourselves when we find and exercise our overdrive gear - our GRIT. GRIT now becomes the cement between the small spaces within the life jar.

Often, we grow most in our leadership when we lead through difficult or challenging times. As leaders, we need to find another gear to be able to manage, persevere, and rise above these times. Usually, these times are the UN-demands on our leadership: unexpected, unplanned, and most certainly unwanted, but because we are leaders, we have no other choice than to confront them. To do so, we must find our overdrive gear of GRIT that can push us past what we think is our limited capacity to extend beyond the unimaginable limits of our capacity. This takes GRIT, and possessing GRIT liberates and empowers a leader. . With the visual illustration now complete, we move to discuss ways we manage ourselves when we feel our life jar is beyond capacity.

> **MAKE YOUR OWN CHANGE**
>
> **IF YOU WANT SOMETHING YOU'VE NEVER HAD, YOU MUST BE WILLING TO DO SOMETHING YOU'VE NEVER DONE**
>
> **THOMAS JEFFERSON**

The great leadership teacher, STEVEN COVEY, author of Seven Habits of Highly Effective People said about life balance, "the key is not to prioritize what's on your schedule, but to schedule your priorities." This is a clear and crucial reminder for us to keep the main thing the main thing. Some leaders have the luxury of a personal assistant who creates and coordinates their executive schedules. Doing so keeps the leader's time focused on essential tasks. I do not have the luxury of a personal assistant, so I need to put mechanisms in place. If I don't, distractions pull me away from my 'main thing.' What do you do to help you keep the main thing the main thing?

One tactic to maintain focus is easily remembered by the acronym **SOBER** which stands for Schedule, Organize, Balance, Encourage, and Relax.

S is for SCHEDULE: Many top leaders spend time determining the things that will keep them focused on their main thing by identifying all the other things that are pulling on their time demand. It begins with clearly identifying the essential priorities to fit into your life jar (golf balls) but also consider the things represented by pebbles too! The key is to make a conscious effort to decide thoughtfully and intentionally what to focus on at any given moment. If we don't, then we tend to waste time thinking we are busy, but instead spin our wheels aimlessly. On a macro level we must be able to identify major and minor priorities in our life. On a micro level we must identify and plan for the UN-demands that are unexpected and unwanted while conserving the overdrive GRIT energy we need to intentionally be available for pleasure. If we manage our schedule effectively we begin to harness the elusive element of time and help keep our main thing the main thing without sacrificing all the other things we need in life. Take a few minutes to thoughtfully and intentionally identify the macro and micro items in your life jar that need to be scheduled.

O is for ORGANIZE: Being able to organize means one must be able to identify the values that will guide our selection process. Why do some put religion or faith above other things? Because that is where they put a high value need for their life. Some may wake up and immediately exercise before the tasks of the day take over their time demand. These individuals have set the value of health and exercise as a priority, and so they organize their time to honor that value. I have found that taking a few minutes at the beginning or end of the day to organize the upcoming day is a valuable exercise for me. When done through the lens of setting my intention to honor what I value I ensure that I build in the time to fulfill those values that guide my time. Are you able to identify your values so that you can better organize your time and energy?

B is for BALANCE: Balance is the ability to keep all of the things you carry in a steady position so you don't fall over. With so many tugs and pulls on our time and energy the ability to balance will involve our mental and physical strength and conditioning. For some, they find balance within a strict routine. The regiment of routine helps them keep focused and heading in a desired direction. Others choose to balance based on feelings. Others use the life-support system. They apply their life-support focus to the area that is hemorrhaging the most at the moment. Know and understand how you achieve balance so that you can evaluate the success or failure of your system. Recognize that we all have personal wants and needs that must be met. Starving one want or need to feed another is not the same as finding balance. We must know what we value and understand how we balance so that we feed all of our wants and needs. How do you balance your wants and needs?

E is for ENCOURAGE: As mentioned in the previous chapter about the power of positive messages we all need to feel as if we have a champion rooting for us in life. We need the encouragement of others, and when we receive this encouragement the impact is appreciated. Of course, we balance this with the understanding that it is equally as helpful when we are also a champion for others. The reciprocity in encouragement helps feed and grow the love and connection we have with others. To whom can you be a champion? Who is your champion to whom you will offer your power of positive messages? As leaders we need to do this for those we lead, but we also need to receive encouragement as well. Leaders often struggle with giving or receiving encouragement. They either find it hard to encourage others or forget to accept the encouragement from those around them. Who is your champion? Who claims you as their champion?

R is for RELAX: Admittedly, I have found this to be a need that takes a concentrated effort to ensure it gets fed. Understanding how we like to relax is as important as taking time to relax. There are many who find curling up with a book on a rainy-day relaxing. Others find a quiet stroll in nature's solitude to be an important part of their ability to relax. For those of us who are true extroverts, we may find being in the company of others equally as relaxing and rejuvenating. Still, others may need to do a total shut off and shut down to find their full relaxation mode. When the life jar feels full or even overflowing it may be necessary to find how you can best relax in order to recharge. Only then can you kick it into the overdrive GRIT gear. What do you do to relax? Do you relax enough?

As stated earlier in the book, leadership is influence. To be effective leaders we must first be effective in influencing ourselves so that we can also effectively influence others. In my leadership training sessions I talk a lot about Emotional Intelligence (EQ). EQ is essential to understanding how we manage our emotions. Balancing our life jar is relative to how we handle and process our own emotions necessary for self-management. Our EQ does not only impact how we see and treat ourselves, but also how we see and treat others. Recognizing, understanding, and managing our own emotions is a prerequisite for being able to recognize, understand, and influence the emotional maturity in others. Successfully keeping the main thing the main thing is tightly connected to our EQ and not simply a time management issue. By being able to keep the main thing the main things we increase our effectiveness and ability to lead and influence others.

YOUR LIFE JAR
IS YOUR JAR AT CAPACITY?
WHAT CAN YOU DO BETTER TO KEEP THE MAIN THING THE MAIN THING?

Knowledge is simply good advice waiting to be given, but worthless if you keep it to yourself.

Chapter 5: FROM RAGS TO RICHES—FINDING PASSION & PURPOSE

You may have figured out by now that I love a good story. Whether it is from a movie, a book, or one that is retold, I thoroughly enjoy learning how people overcome seemingly insurmountable odds to achieve things greater than what they, or others, thought possible. I find these stories inspirational because if they were able to do it then maybe I might be able to capture some of their positive power as well. In my own pursuit of improving myself and my leadership skills I find stories of human success and achievement to be empowering and motivational.

I recently came across an old family photo from a newspaper when my father had become the pastor at Church of the Open Door in York, Pennsylvania. I had not seen this photo for many years, so I found myself gazing at the photo for quite some time. This picture captured how my family looked more than 50 years ago! Yes, that is me in the fancy striped jacket shaking hands with the man in the photo. To my right is my sister Linda. Next to her is my late-brother David, and sisters Barbara and Ginny. My beloved parents (David and Roxie Haines, both of whom have passed away, stand behind us.

The Haines family 1969

I was the youngest of five children. As the youngest, my siblings will probably tell you that I got away with everything while they got caught for everything. The truth of that statement continues to be a debate amongst my siblings over shared holiday meals. I remind them that by the time mom and dad got through raising them they were so burned out and tired that I simply did not draw the same level of attention that my brother and sisters did. After all, I was the good child. Looking back on this photo, one curious question remains: did the little boy in the photo have any idea what he would become or would want to become when he grew up? I do recall sharing at around this age that I wanted to be an ice cream man, not because I could earn a living at it, but because I loved eating it. I thought it would be an awesome job because then I could eat it any time I wanted to.

My passion for eating ice cream never did materialize into a career, but, then again, neither did my passion for football lead me to play in the National Football League. I do not feel a sense of disappointment for not accomplishing those childhood dreams, especially since my private high school didn't even have a football team. However, when I was fifteen years old, I had a teacher that would reshape the direction of my life. Don Martindell was a young twenty-six-year-old teacher new to my school. Plumstead Christian School was a small private school that had just gone through a building expansion program that added classrooms, administrative offices, and a new gymnasium. Don was hired to be the Athletic Director, PE teacher, history teacher, and after school sports coach. I am sure he wanted his first day of school to be memorable, and the events in his first history class did not disappoint. After finishing the pleasantries of a personal introduction, he jumped right into a motivational speech about our 9th grade civics class overview. In a moment of dramatic presentation as he attempted to stand up from his teaching stool the foot rungs broke, sending him sprawling onto the floor. Who doesn't love a good laugh at someone else's falling expense? My classmates and I blurted out a loud and jolly laughter. Mr. Martindell did not find the situation nearly as funny as we did. Visibly mad, but probably more embarrassed, this was not the first day memories or impression he was hoping to establish. I am glad to say that he and I have shared many laughs over that moment through the years, and I am grateful that his passion and influence inspired me to pursue a career working with children.

When Don was a young child he probably had no idea of the future impact he would have students like me. I recently came across a photo of a young Jack Ma Yun. Having traveled many times to China, I am well aware of his success with Alibaba. I became curious as to the events in his life that may have contributed to him becoming a successful mega-billionaire businessman. Growing up in China, Jack Ma was under the same academic pressures as many other Chinese students. For the student, the demand for high grades and exam scores opens or closes educational doors of opportunity. Ma's hopes of attending a well-respected university seemed unreachable because he failed his university entrance exam twice and was rejected by Harvard University ten times. The chance for advanced academic success seemed elusive and out of reach, so Ma decided to get a job. His work success did not fare any better than his academics. Ma was rejected from dozens of jobs he applied for including his attempt to work at KFC! When KFC came to China, twenty four people showed up and

> **YOUR PASSION IS YOUR NORTH STAR**
>
> **ALWAYS REMEMBER YOU HAVE WITHIN YOU THE STRENGTH, THE PATIENCE, AND THE PASSION TO REACH FOR THE STARS AND CHANGE THE WORLD.**
>
> **HARRIET TUBMAN**

applied for a job, and twenty three of them were hired. got one. Ma was the only one turned away. However, always maintaining a positive outlook, Ma chose to build upon his strengths, and speaking English was one of them. With newfound confidence and direction, he decided to become an English teacher at a local university where he was paid a salary of about 100 RMB per month, equal to about twenty US dollars. Forever the optimist, Ma recalls those teaching years as the "best days of his life."

Ma was driven by his curiosity to consider the changes taking place in the world because of access to internet technology. Without any formal training he tried launching some early technology companies, but each failed. Relying on his GRIT, he chose to press on. Four years later he experienced a life changing event when he invited seventeen of his friends inside his small apartment to hear his next entrepreneurial vision. Unfazed and unrestrained by previous failure, Ma convinced his friends to invest in his vision for an online marketplace he would call "Alibaba." Currently, the value of Alibaba is closing in on $200 billion. The young boy with few academic choices and a few failed business attempts utilized his GRIT to endure. At the age of 54, Jack Ma announced he would step down as CEO of Alibaba and return to "the best days of his life," his original passion for teaching.

Ma was born in October of 1964, so he is only 2-months older than I am. I think I love his story so much because if you study his pursuit to find passion and purpose it is not just about making money. It was also not just to establish his business as a massive global enterprise or to even become one of the world's wealthiest individuals. His passion was to pursue his curiosity and his purpose was driven by personal goals that were closely guarded by a fierce determination, steady perseverance, and remarkable resiliency. When asked why he stepped down from the CEO position to teach, Ma said, "we cannot teach our kids to compete with the machines who are smarter—we have to teach our kids something unique. In this way, thirty years later, kids will have a chance." Ma remains steadfast in his original passion and purpose: people, not the accumulation of things, occupy the forefront of his vision.

Finding your passion and purpose is a worthwhile venture. For me, I feel fortunate that at the age of fifteen my teacher and coach inspired me to work with children. I continue to set my life's goals around this passion and purpose. I found that through teaching middle school students I was able to influence my students through some of those awkward and difficult teen years. Importantly, I was able to connect with them as people, and as I evolved and matured I simply found other economic ways to pursue my passion and purpose of connecting with children by creating educational opportunities in school and in summer camp.

Finding passion and purpose may take a lifetime or it may happen by the age of fifteen. There seems to be no formula to predict when it is found, but it is important we remain on the lookout for what that might be for each of us. Passion is "how" you do something, and purpose is "why" you do something. Knowing your how and why provides a laser focus and helps you keep the main thing the main thing. Until you have a grasp of your passion and purpose, you need to keep pursuing your highest curiosity and remain vigilant to discover where that leads you.

I would like to share a few steps that might help you, or those you lead, find passion and purpose. These points come from the master mentor Jack Canfield, a legend in the field of motivational speaking.

EXPLORE THINGS—Adopt the mind and will of an explorer. Be willing to venture into parts unknown and unfamiliar to you. Treat your new interests like an uncharted and unconquered frontier. Too many of us never get out of our comfort zone, choosing instead to live and die inside the safe parameters we establish for ourselves. We can learn from those who boldly blaze new trails, accepting the risks and rewards that may come from trying something for the first time. Why not be the explorer that others choose to talk about? Those who are brave enough to commit to the pursuit with GRIT will likely discover what they are hoping to find.

TAKE LIFE INVENTORY— Knowing who you are and what you want to become is essential to discovering your passion and purpose. Determine your strengths, weaknesses and interests. Knowing this is vital to your self-discovery process. If you are not perceptive enough to identify these within yourself, then make sure you find an honest friend or mentor who would be willing to help you take a self-inventory so you can begin to discover what they may see in you.

CREATE A LIFE STATEMENT- A life statement is your purpose of intent in how you will choose to live. This statement will serve as a beacon to guide your search for passion and purpose. A life statement is at the essence of who you are and at the core of what you believe. Your life statement will encompass your values embedded within your motivation for pursuing your purpose. *See an example of a Life Statement at the end of this chapter.

CHOOSE GUIDANCE CAREFULLY—Everyone needs a mentor and a champion. Rarely one may find a single person in his or her life that can serve as both. Know the difference between these two roles. The Champion will cheer you on in every occasion, and the mentor will help redirect you with painful honesty when you need it. A mentor may not always cheer for you, but he or she should always be honest with you. Again, it is possible for one individual in your life to serve as both your champion and your mentor. Knowing who you can trust to fulfill these roles for you is important.

DECIDED DETERMINATION—Finding the intersection of purpose and passion is a search worth taking. When you find it, you feel the peace that comes from resting in your "sweet spot of life." It doesn't mean you will live a problem-free or stress-free life but living with passion and purpose is full of great satisfaction. Do not stop the pursuit. Do not let a current job or economic status be the thing that halts your search. Be vigilant and full of decided determination.

It feels good to dream, but it feels much better when our dreams come true. I don't think people spend enough time dreaming anymore. At age fifteen, my dreaming took a positive turn because of the passion and purpose I saw lived out by one teacher. His example and inspiration helped change the trajectory of my life. Fortunately, my teacher was not my only example of someone living a passionate and purposeful life. When my father was young he made a similar commitment to be the best Bible teacher he could be. He approached his work with passion, and he aligned that passion with the purpose to teach and guide those who were part of his churches. Similarly, my father-in-law also followed his passion to pursue his purpose to do the exact same thing my father did. I was blessed to have such leaders in my life.

After taking another look back at the early childhood photo shown at the start of this chapter, I certainly see myself and my siblings without a care or worry in the world. We were young, and we were clothed, fed, and housed by two loving parents. My focus on the photo shifts from the children and onto my parents. In that photo my father was a young man of forty-three. He stands proudly with his wife and the five children they both loved deeply. My father made a commitment to actively search for his purpose and passion, and he was divinely inspired to teach others. He faithfully served his purpose with great passion and love for over 50 years. He chose to forsake higher paying jobs because he was committed to a life lived at the intersection of passion and purpose. My father inspired me.

If you have not yet ventured out in an earnest search for that intersection in your own life, maybe start by asking yourself the following questions:

Why did I stop dreaming big?

What sense of purpose do I bring those I lead?

Who inspires me, and what is it about them I should emulate?

When you stop dreaming, you start dying. Some say 'dream big' or in the words of Steve D. Sims "dream stupid!" Meaning, be willing to dream so big that it almost sounds stupid. If you stopped dreaming, start again. When you find the intersection of passion and purpose you will rest in the shade of a peace that will calm your soul.

> **DID YOU STOP DREAMING?**
>
> **WHAT CHILDHOOD DREAM DID YOU HAVE FOR YOURSELF?**
>
> **WHAT EVIDENCE OF PASSION DO YOU BRING TO YOUR CURRENT JOB?**

Knowledge is simply good advice waiting to be given, but worthless if you keep it to yourself.

*Developing your personal life statement.

Writing a personal life (mission) statement serves as a mission statement that will be the standard by which everything you say and do will be measured and directed. Although putting something in writing feels permanent to many, the life statement may change and evolve as you change and evolve. However, the process of writing it and living with it is valuable to your personal and leadership growth.

If you follow Steven Covey's 7 Habits mission statement ideas, it will be centered on the core values of who you are and who you want to become. This mission statement can serve you as a guide through the many phases and changes in life. While your mission statement may be amended as you yourself evolve, crystallizing the changeless core of who you are will actually help you adapt to change. This is because it reinforces a secure sense of self that won't be threatened by changes around you. The process of writing your mission statement is just as important as the final product. The development process will force you to think through how you want to live your life and what actions you will take to accomplish your personal goals.

The ideas shared above came from a summary article based on Steven Covey's model in his 7 Habits book.

Your 7 habits mission statement should focus on three things:

Character: Who do you want to be?

Contribution: What do you want to do?

Achievements: What are the core values and principles that govern your character and contributions?

Find value in the process as well as the product. Make the process therapeutic and dig deep into your thoughts and ideas to generate your statement. I happily share my current personal mission statement with you. I wrote my original version 10 years ago, but I have revised it into its current form and, because I have grown as a person through significant personal and professional experiences and life changes.

I will live in humility and with contentment but refuse to become complacent or restless. I choose to demonstrate and vocalize my gratitude in all situations, good and bad, as I realize life lessons may be learned in all situations. I strive with sincerity to love others without the need or expectation of what may or may not be given in return. In all situations I will remain steadfastly grounded in my faith—firmly gripping the full assurance that I am guided by God who loves me and will not give me more than I can carry.

May this always be true of me.

    Steve Haines

Chapter 6: THE POWER OF MOMENTS

I can still recall the beautiful clear and cloudless blue sky as I commuted to my teaching job with my children in the car. After making my ritualistic stop at Starbucks I was now loaded with the power of caffeine to face the challenges of another day of middle school teaching. After arriving at school all seemed normal as I greeted my 8th grade class with a big smile. This was only the 2nd full day of classes at the start of the year, and I was frantically trying to learn all their names. I noticed their smiles, and I heard their excited laughter. It was easy to imagine the adventures this school year would hold for all of us. The recurring start to every 8th grade school year was a planned and much anticipated whole class camping trip set to begin the next day. My intent today was to spend a few minutes talking about my positive hopes for the school year and then, when the other half of 8th grade was finished with their class, we would gather as a whole grade to handle some logistical planning for the camping trip. This camping trip was highly anticipated because it was a trip that every middle school student looked forward to in their 8th grade final year of middle school. The goal of the trip was to bond together through a few nights of sleeping in tents, making our own meals, hiking in nature, and playing lots of fun games and activities. My colleagues and I looked forward to the trip as much as the students did.

Having given what I thought was an inspirational speech about setting their personal goals for the year; reinforcing the class culture of respect for self, others, the school, and learning, I realized that I still had 15 minutes before the other section of the class joined us. I decided to turn the television on to burn up the final few minutes before our class meeting was to begin. In 2001, my classroom was one of the few with a television that was connected to cable to receive CNN news. So, at about 8:50 AM I grabbed the remote and turned on the news. To the horror of all, we saw the North Tower of the World Trade Center billowing with smoke. Mesmerized by shock, we sat watching the horrific events unfold as the 2nd plane flew into the South Tower. When this happened on September 11, 2001, life suddenly changed, and we all felt vulnerable and uneasy. The power of this moment is forever etched into the minds of everyone who saw these horrific events unfold.

Why is it that certain moments in life are so memorable—never forgotten—while other moments are simply forgotten? Why with certain events can I remember the clear and cloudless blue sky even though I have lived under thousands of cloudless blue skies in my lifetime? Why is it that I remember where I was at the moment of the terrorist attacks of September 11, 2001, with a degree of clarity and recall, but I am likely unable to recall what I ate yesterday for lunch? The fact is we do not remember days, but we do remember certain moments.

I read a great book by Chip and Dan Heath called The Power of Moments (Oct. 2017). I highly recommend the book for any teacher or leader. It was a transformational book for me, helping to reshape my ideas on leadership and connection to those I lead. I hope you find it as powerful as I did.

This book uncovers some fascinating mysteries of why some experiences in life are remembered differently than others. It provides evidence as to why we tend to remember the best moments, the worst moments and the last moments of an experience while often forgetting the rest. Why "we feel most comfortable when things are certain, but we feel most alive when they're not." If we think carefully we can categorize various life events—some with greater detail and impact than others. Understanding why this occurs is a valuable and fascinating study. Inspired by this book, I call these occasions "M & M Moments" in life because they are Memorable and Meaningful Moments.

There are great lessons in leadership to be found in how we remember and embrace our M & M Moments. These memorable and meaningful moments do not just have to be serendipitous moments outside of our control. In understanding the full impact of the power of moments we can harness the power through intentional design and creation of such moments for ourselves and for those we lead. In doing so, we add to our influence and effectiveness as a leader.

We remember moments because of our connection to them. Maybe we recall the sights, sounds, and smells, or maybe we recall the faces, features, and facts that make up these M & M Moments. The key is in the word 'experience.' Reading about such moments does NOT have the same impact as when you live in the moment.

> **POWER OF MOMENTS**
>
> **THE 'OCCASSIONALLY REMARKABLE' MOMENTS SHOULDN'T BE LEFT TO CHANCE! THEY SHOULD BE PLANNED FOR, INVESTED IN. THEY ARE PEAKS THAT SHOULD BE BUILT. AND IF WE FAIL TO DO THAT, LOOK AT WHAT WE'RE LEFT WITH: MOSTLY FORGETTABLE**
>
> **CHIP & DAN HEATH**

Authors of the book, Chip and Dan Heath, use a helpful acronym of the word EPIC so we know better how to focus on the intentional creation of M & M Moments.

E is for Elevation: Moments are powerful when they are moments like no other. These special moments of elevation are "above and beyond" the normal moments of life we experience. We won't remember walking into a Starbucks for coffee unless one day we entered and ran into a very famous celebrity. Then, we are likely to remember much about that experience. I may not remember all the dates I have had with my wife, but I will not forget our wedding day. My wedding day was burned into my mind as a moment of high elevation. It was clearly a day and date well outside the normal, everyday experience. A moment that is elevated higher than any other typical moment is likely to become an M & M Moment. Elevation is the first important key in making an experience an M & M Moment. To be an elevated moment, it must be a moment outside the normal and everyday occurrence.

P is for Pride: These are moments that occur when we are at our best. We all love to feel good about what we do, who we are, or the achievements and accomplishments we earn. Receiving recognition or praise elevates the pride we have in ourselves. Chip and Dan Heath found that we remember moments more when our pride is stroked. I can recall when I was in the 5th grade and I won "run the bases" and the 100-yard dash at my end of school year event. Because it was a moment of great personal pride, some of the details surrounding the event are more pronounced than other events I ran in. In fact, I remember everything about my wardrobe that day: an orange Orioles shirt, shorts, and yes, tube socks complete with black and orange stripes to match my Orioles shirt. Had I finished 3rd or 4th, I doubt I would recall anything about the day. The ribbon and the trophy I earned stroked my pride and made that moment an M & M Moment for me. We remember M & M Moments when we feel proud of our accomplishments or when others recognize our accomplishments. M & M Moments are moments that fill us with pride.

I is for Insight: This element is often the most difficult to observe. Insight elements are often referred to as "ah-ha" moments. New insights expand our understanding of something and cause us to think differently about something.ng As a teacher, I remember moments when a particular student was struggling to grasp a concept that I was teaching. Seeing their visible frustration I would try to work with that student in hopes that I might explain it differently so that they could grasp the concept or idea. Often the time I invested would produce a moment of recognition for the student—a moment when the "light" comes on and they finally understand the initial concept. An M & M Moment is more likely to occur when it is a moment that produces new insight and when we think or act differently for being in that moment or experience.

C is for Connection: To me, this is the most significant element in establishing an M & M Moment. I am a person who needs people around me, so any opportunity for deeper connection is meaningful to me. I am an extrovert, and I find energy and strength from being around others. Many of my M & M Moments in life are closely tied to the people I was with at that moment of the experience. In my young college days, I formed a rock-n-roll band with my college roommate. We wrote songs, recorded demos, played concerts, and enjoyed some regional success for more than 10 years. I can recall our first concert because it was a special moment to take the stage for the very first time. But I also recall aspects of other shows based on moments with my bandmates, the crowd reaction, or other elements related to who I may have felt connected with at that show. Often, moments become M & M Moments and can be remembered because of who joined us in sharing that experience. It is the same reason why teammates who won a sports championship together feel forever bonded because of that accomplishment together as a team. The same feeling of connection would likely be shared by a rescuer and the person rescued. Often a deep bond of connection is forged because of the experience both shared in that memorable event. Connection contributes greatly to making special moments memorable and meaningful.

Supported by their research findings, the Heath brothers conclude that when multiple EPIC elements are present in an experience there is a far greater chance that the experience will be remembered. If we understand the elements of EPIC that make up the power of moments could there also be an advantage if we could work to intentionally create or manufacture more of these moments? Would the ability to intentionally increase these moments also add to our influence as a leader? What if a teacher-leader could intentionally create M & M

Moments in the context of learning information at school? Couldn't that be a win-win for both teacher and the learners?

I have been blessed to travel to China many times in my work as an International Education Consultant. I consider those trips to be full of amazing memories, but sadly, not all are remembered. I mean, one cannot walk on the Great Wall of China, or walk in and around Beijing, Shanghai, or Shenzhen and not appreciate the wonders seen. Those moments are enhanced when sitting around a large round table with others eating the delicious cuisine that China is noted for. I find the sights, sounds, smells, and tastes are only enhanced by the connections shared with others in those moments. In that, I am like many learners I taught: if you show or tell me something I might remember part of it. However, if you involve me in doing something my retention, and therefore my recall, is far greater. I have tried to apply this understanding of myself into my teacher training funshops.

I love games and activities that make me laugh and are fun to participate in. As a result, I implement many such activities within my training funshops. It is not only a great diversion and change of pace after sitting for a while, but also it tends to be within those activities where deeper and more meaningful connections to the participants and the information are better formed and established. When the participants interact with others, relax, laugh, and move and this active learning helps reinforce the information learned, the experience is more fun for me and for them, and the connection to the material is better emphasized.

Teachers and leaders need to do more to engage the participant because this is what helps solidify experiences into long-term memories. This was emphasized recently when I came across one of the Chinese teachers who participated in my training funshops. She posted a video on her WeChat app of one of the group-building activities we did in the workshop. I believe because she participated in this active learning she more easily recalled what she had learned. Experiences are more meaningful when we are an engaged participant, and engaged participants more easily remember the lessons.

One of the worst pitfalls for any leader is complacency. When we become complacent, we become lazy. Suddenly the routine becomes a rut, and to steer out of the rut takes more energy than we are willing to commit to the task. I call it the "rut routine," and it is a horrible place to exist. I see many leaders fall into the rut routine, and it often leads to a slow and suffocating leadership death. For the teacher-leader, it means they stop trying new ways to enhance their teaching strategies. For the business leader they begin to take for granted their client base and what they appreciate most about them or the product. Suddenly we become stale and stagnant, and this evokes complacency. Avoiding complacency keeps us on the cutting edge of effectiveness and away from the rut routine. Obviously, we all have some routines that are comforting. But I am talking about the routines in our leadership that weaken, not strengthen, us as leaders. If you cannot see them in yourself, be sure to empower those around you (e.g. your mentors) to point them out so you are not a victim of the rut routine. When we seek to master how we celebrate or even intentionally create memorable moments for ourselves or those we lead, we begin to learn how to harness the advantages through the power of moments.

Add EPIC Moments To Your Leadership Influence

"We don't remember days, we remember moments." How many intentional M & M Moments can you create for those you lead? Do you see how creating these M & M Moments would make you a more effective and influential leader? I hope the answer to the first question is many, and I hope the answer to the second question is yes! If so, congratulations! I would bet that your influence as a leader is strong and healthy. But for those who cannot honestly answer each of these questions in this way, I want to give you some tips to consider so you can embrace the impact that the power of moments can have on you and on those you lead.

Take some personal reflection time and consider how you might add intentional M & M Moments for those you lead. Plan a special party of recognition for those who have been working at a high level. Do not just say "good job," but be specific in what you see in their work performance or in what has contributed to their success. Write handwritten notes or deliver a speech of recognition. Make the event special by inviting their spouses or significant others to hear the praise. Give them a gift to commemorate the event. Top it off with music, balloons, or special food to help give it even greater flare. By seeking to tap into multiple elements of EPIC you elevate the overall impact of the power of this moment. Leadership takes an intentional attitude and intentional work. Use the intention to get out of the rut routine.

Create an M & M committee. Creating an M & M committee helps share the responsibilities of looking for and intentionally creating events. The committee can also be tasked with looking to make the power of the moment known. The collective ideas and responsibilities can be more easily shared amongst others. The committee may track milestone moments, births or birthdays, accomplishments to be recognized, anniversaries, or work anniversaries. Recognize important events to emphasize them as moments worthy of attention. Seek to make these moments memorable and special. Doing this by committee shares the burden and creates greater buy in from others.

Do not let the unplanned go unnoticed. Many M&M Moments happen serendipitously and without planning. However, just because they were not known about or pre-planned doesn't mean they should go by unnoticed. Be prepared to celebrate the moment. You may not have time to order food, balloons, music, etc., but even a quick handwritten note, an announcement, or focused recognition is better than doing nothing. Have some special things on hand specifically for different types of moments and occasions. Just like a teacher that might have stickers or lollipops to celebrate a student's success, have something at the ready so the moment is celebrated instead of unnoticed.

Connect with those you lead. Many leaders seem to feel that if they connect too closely with those whom they lead their leadership respect will be compromised. I respectfully disagree with that. I believe the deeper the genuine connection we have with those we lead the more apt a leader we become. The more we know those whom we lead, the less likely we will be surprised by moments. Depending on the size of your company it may not be possible to know each and every person, but if you have a management or leadership team in place, you can let them know you want them to be on the lookout for opportunities to intentionally celebrate moments that are important to those being led.

> **CREATE A MEMORABLE & MEANINGFUL MOMENT**
>
> **PICK SOMEONE YOU WANT TO BLESS WITH AN M & M MOMENT YOU WILL CREATE. WHO WILL IT BE FOR, AND HOW WILL YOU MAKE THE MOMENT E.P.I.C. ?**

Connection builds community. It doesn't weaken it. Connecting with those you lead is likely to reveal so many additional power-of-moment opportunities to share together as a school or company.

Get out of the rut routine. Although easier said than done, you must remember that complacency got you into the rut and only intentional hard work will get you out. Select a few key team members that you can share what has put your leadership into a rut routine and equip them with the task of accountability to help you get out. If you are not sure how to identify the rut you are in, you should invest in a leadership coach to help expose that for you. Swallow the pride and be the change necessary to build your influence. Those you lead will respect you for it!

The goal for any leader is to effectively influence others. Those we lead want to be appreciated, honored, and recognized just like you do as a leader. If we know what elements help make some moments more memorable and meaningful, then we can increase our influence if we take the time to celebrate. When we invest in harnessing the power of moments, we expand our influence and show appreciation for others as we work to make the moment for them as powerful as we possibly can. Create a life full of M & M Moments. You won't regret it.

Knowledge is simply good advice waiting to be given, but worthless if you keep it to yourself.

Chapter 7: LEARNING TO FAIL BETTER THAN ANYONE ELSE

When was the last time you failed at something? How did it make you feel? Consider these two heroic failure stories. During his lifetime, this artist suffered mental illness, had failed relationships, and sadly committed suicide at the young age of 37. While alive he was considered a failed artist because he only managed to sell a handful of paintings and even had to trade some of his art in exchange for medical

> **WHAT IS YOUR MINDSET REGARDING FAILURE?**
>
> I CAN ACCEPT FAILURE; EVERYONE FAILS AT SOMETHING. BUT I CANNOT ACCEPT NOT TRYING.
>
> MICHAEL JORDAN

treatment. Having famously cut his ear off in an argument with fellow artist, Paul Gauguin, the Dutch painter ended up in an asylum where he spent over a year. Although considered to be a commercial failure, Vincent Van Gough did not stop painting. Regrettably, he would never realize that years after his death he would become known as a key artist figure in the world of post-impressionism art. Today, he is one of the most recognized artists in the world. Among his famous paintings, **Portrait du Docteur Gachet** sold for a record $75 million dollars. Van Gough never learned how to fail.

Readers were swept away back in 1997 with the captivating story of Harry Potter and his adventures at Hogwarts School of Witchcraft and Wizardry. But Harry Potter fans were amazed to learn about author J.K. Rawling's humble beginnings which were far different from where she now sits as one of the world's most esteemed story tellers. Rawling recalls, *"I had failed on an epic scale. An exceptionally short-lived marriage had imploded, and I was jobless, a lone parent, and as poor as possible to be in modern Britain, without being homeless. The fears that my parents had for me, and that I had for myself, had both come to pass, and by every usual standard, I was the biggest failure I knew."* Today, J.K. Rowling has gone on to sell over 500 million books.

These are two contrasting stories about failure. Van Gough by all accounts was so troubled by his failure that suicide seemed like the best solution. On the other hand, amid Rowling's epic failure, she opted to persevere through the bleakest times of life and ended up rising to the top as one of the world's greatest writers. Both failed but each handled their failure fundamentally different from the other. We all experience failure at some time in our life. How we handle failure in leadership, will be part of our legacy of leadership. How we handle our failure in life, will be our life legacy and contribute to how we will be remembered. Like Rowling, I have decided that I want to learn how to fail better than anyone else.

No one sets out with failure as the goal or objective. Humans are not wired to pursue failure, but admittedly there are times our pursuit does end up in what we or others consider failure. Data from the Bureau of Labor Statistics shows that approximately 20% of new businesses fail during the first two years of being open. That failure rate escalates to 45% during the span of the first five years, and 65% during the first 10-year span. Only 25% of new businesses make it to 15 years or more. It is unlikely that any such business opened with the goal or expectation of failure and demise.

In 2014, I bought a family entertainment business. Up to that point, my career had been working in and around the child and family space so when this opportunity came up that specialized in birthday parties, family events, or just a fun place for those seeking to have a little fun with arcades or games, I thought it might be a profitable opportunity to invest in. With hard work, blood, sweat, tears, and of course money, we slowly began to turn the business into something that appeared to be on the success track. Five years in we felt as if the right systems were in place and we managed to avoid the previously mentioned, yet gloomy statistic of new business failure. After enjoying some of the best revenue months ever, the global pandemic COVID-19 came, and the nosedive business crash was quick and lethal. The Pennsylvania Governor ordered business to close and just like that, the phone to book new parties and events stopped ringing, only to be replaced by the property owner who started calling and demanding his full rent. Being forced to predict the incredibly unstable future and duration of the pandemic impact, we decided to take the necessary steps to close our business and liquidate the assets. Just like that, we went from riding high optimism to part of the 65% failure statistic after just 7 years. We are wired to seek success but when failure comes, how we handle it will determine a lot about our leadership maturity and certainly our emotional stability and resolve.

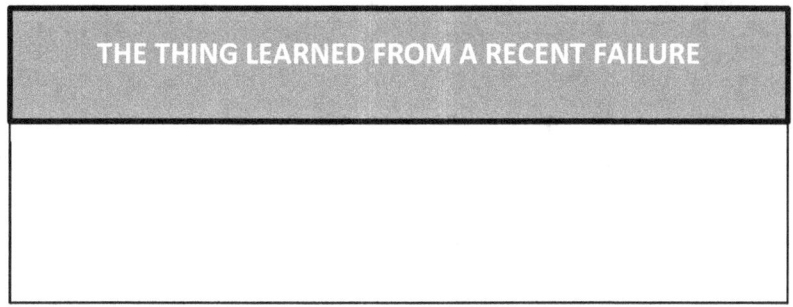

This specific business closure is certainly not my only failure in life. In my book, **The Art of Facilitation: Discovery of the Group Growth Process** (2020), I candidly talk about my childhood failure in baseball. I begged my parents to let me play community baseball, and I was "drafted" and placed with other 9-year-old boys on the ORIOLES! Growing up in York, Pennsylvania at the time, the Baltimore Orioles were my hometown team. Nothing seemed better than to play on a Little League team named after my favorite team. I eagerly took to the ball field with the goal that I would emulate the great Orioles' third baseman Brooks Robinson, the famed shortstop Mark Belanger, or any of the other famous heroes I watched and admired from my home team. However, when it came to having the skill to play baseball, I was anything but a star. In fact, I was terrible!

I did not get a hit the entire season. Imagine playing twelve games in a season and batting three to four times a game with absolutely no hits! The only time I got on base was when I was hit in the head by a pitch. By all baseball standards, I was a failure.

Following my own epic failure consistently on display in front of family and fans, my father gave me some great advice: "Steve, you are not very good at baseball. Maybe you should try another sport." Hearing my father say those words hurt, but it was the right and perfect advice for me to hear. Most parents, afraid to crush dreams and hurt feelings, might advise their child to give it another try, or to work and practice harder, or maybe to stick with it and never quit. But instead, his words moved me to pursue soccer and basketball. I later went on to be good enough to play at the university level and played a contributing role in my team winning three NCCAA Division II National Soccer Championships. Accepting my baseball failure provided an opportunity for redirection and refocus. Not only did I play at university level, but I then went on to a lengthy teaching career where I also coached middle school students in basketball, soccer, and tennis. It was the lessons I learned, propelled through failure, which contributed most to my professional life. I learned how to fail better than others because I accepted the failure, redirected my focus, and took on the risk exposure to pursue a new path.

Living with failure is not fun, but it is something we all must figure out how to handle because life is full of disappointments. Failure may not be our intent, and hopefully it also not a frequent occurrence, but I would say it is inevitable. So, how can we learn to fail better than others? I try to teach my own children not to fear failure. Instead, we should fear never having the opportunity to experience failure. With each failure, we have an opportunity for growth and new understanding. I believe having that perspective helps us learn how to face the failure with optimism, personal growth, and leadership development.

I have met many brave leaders who openly share their experiences of failure. Many of these stories are heartbreaking—full of low moments in life when their pride was assaulted and their will to push on was challenged. Some lost every earthly possession in the failure yet were able to reestablish and rebuild to experience the rewards that success can bring. Some, although not losing everything, certainly felt the emotional pain of failure. Regardless of the level of failure, pain was the emotional and often physical result for falling short of their intended goals and expectations. As leaders, it is important that we help those we lead to know how to fail better than anyone else. We can show empathy, but also provide inspiration for having endured our own times of failure.

Five Tips For Failing Better Than Anyone Else

FEEL THE PAIN: In the midst of failure, take a moment to absorb and analyze how you feel. You must make room for your emotions. Pay close attention to the hurt, the disappointment, and the discouragement. The majority of adults are unable to identify their emotions. The sign of an emotionally stable person is someone who can recognize, understand, and manage their own emotions. Earnestly dissect the emotions and feelings and identify what they are so you can understand and manage them moving forward.

THE FIVE-MINUTE RULE: Author and speaker Hal Elrod wrote a great book, Miracle Morning: The 6 Habits That Will Transform Your Life (Before 8 a.m.) In it, Elrod says it is okay to take five minutes and dwell on your pain, anger, sorrow, or whatever emotion you identify. Then, when the timer goes off, he goes on to say that you must realize that what is done is done and that it cannot be changed. Mentally adjust your mindset and begin to focus your energy on the things you can control.

ANALYZE WHAT YOU CAN LEARN: Once the five-minute rule is up, regroup and spend some valuable time analyzing the situation from all angles. As you feel it (and as bad as it may feel), reassure yourself that it will pass. When it does pass, this moment will simply become logged in as a part of your historical perspective. You will emerge better equipped to deal with present and future failure because of it. If you cannot analyze it alone, seek the perspective of a mentor or someone you trust.

LEARN HOW YOU CAN GROW: Just feeling bad about your own failure and analyzing what you can learn from it is not enough. You must process through the stages of feelings and understand what you can do about the failure so that growth, rather than simply failure, can be the outcome. This is where victory over fear comes in. Being able to make it a learning experience gives value to the failure.

STEP BACK UP TO THE PLATE: I told you about my 9-year-old baseball failure. I quit the baseball team after that season, but in my junior year of high school I stepped back up to the plate as a more confident, and slightly more skilled athlete. I would like to tell you that I did not fear failure, but the truth is, even at 17-years old, I trembled just like my 9-year-old self in the orange ORIOLE jersey. I literally swung at the very first pitch which went for a triple. I happily buried my 9-year-old failure on 3rd base that day. Don't let the failure win. Get back up to the plate and take another swing, but this time savor the valuable lessons that failure taught you.

There is a great saying: F-E-A-R either stands for Forget Everything And Run or it means Face Everything And Rise. Which phrase will characterize your mindset when you fail? Can you learn how to fail better than anyone else, or will the failure cause you to drop everything and run away?

Assuming you were born on this planet, it is probable that when I say the name "Michael Jordan," you associate it with one of the best basketball players to ever play the game. Most of us only know MJ when he was on top of his game during his amazing pro basketball career. As a pro, he helped his team win six NBA championships, he earned five League MVPs, and multiple NBA All-Defensive team awards. He sits on top of a short list of elite scorers and probably among the top three all-time greatest players to ever play the game. But even he failed.

> *"I've missed more than 9,000 shots in my career. I've lost almost 300 games. Twenty-six times I've been trusted to take the game winning shot and missed. I've failed over and over and over again in my life. And that is why I succeed."* (Michael Jordan)

Many forget that as a sophomore in high school Michael Jordan was cut from the team because his coach did not think he was good enough. Feeling great pain in failure, Michael analyzed his failure and determined he would Face Everything And Rise. He improved his training, and within five years of that massive failure he led the University of North Carolina Tar Heels to the NCAA Division I National Championship. His perspective of success is deeply rooted in the opportunity he had to fail. Michael Jordan learned how to fail better than anyone else.

The true strength of any leader will be how he or she handles moments of failure. Followers can forgive failure when it is the result of sincere effort and pure motives. They can also forgive failure when victory and defeat are both part of the calculated risk factors. Sadly, we have seen that most people can also forgive a leader's failure when it is the result of greed, immorality, or less than pure motives. We will all experience failure in leadership, but if the fear of failure makes a leader indecisive or apprehensive, the fear of failure can easily cripple a leader. "Successful [people] become successful only because they acquire the habit of thinking in terms of success." (Napoleon Hill). Successful leaders are like successful people. They try to mitigate the risks as much as possible, but they do not let the fear of failure get in the way of pursuing success, even at the cost of failure.

> **WHAT IS YOUR RISK REACTION?**
>
> **WHICH BEST DESCRIBES YOUR MINDSET ABOUT FAILURE?**
>
> ☐ **FORGET EVERYTHING AND RUN**
>
> ☐ **FACE EVERYTHING AND RISE**

Knowledge is simply good advice waiting to be given, but worthless if you keep it to yourself.

Chapter 8:   THE PIN DROP

Have you ever been lost? I mean, really lost? It is a frightening feeling to have no idea where you are or how to get to your intended destination. On one of my travels to China, I found myself lost in Beijing, one of the world's largest cities with an estimated population of over 21 million people. Without the ability to speak or read Mandarin, and without the aid of Google translate, I was wandering in a sea of unfamiliar faces and surroundings. I was lost and lonely even though I was surrounded by plenty of people. Although I was not alone, I was unable to effectively communicate my situation.

Standing on a busy sidewalk with my suitcase in tow and wearing the obvious look of a lost tourist on my face, a sweet Chinese woman and her 5-year-old daughter stopped to see if they could help. Her very poor conversational skills with English far surpassed my own skills in Mandarin, and this gave me hope. Using a lot of non-verbal skills like gestures and pointing she miraculously understood I was looking for the Metro station. With a big smile and some undetectable but confident words spoken in Mandarin, I put my trust in her and proceeded to follow them to the Metro station entrance, just three blocks away. I was profoundly grateful for her help and relieved to be headed in the right direction. It is frightening to be lost, but it is wonderful to be given a lifeline of help and hope.

Our mobile phones are amazing devices. They include tools of efficiency and communication, they possess the ability to capture moments on camera or video, and they keep us connected to people and the internet. Through our phones we can order food, pay bills, order an Uber, keep our calendars, and, of course, make phone calls. There is almost nothing we cannot do through our phones. In fact, when I was lost in Beijing, if I had then the mobile phone that I have now, my adventure of being lost in Beijing would not have been a frightening issue at all. I would have simply opened my Google translate app to assist in my communication. Or, I could have sent a message through WeChat to my Chinese friend who could have easily dropped me a pin exactly where the Metro station was located. It is much harder to be lost these days when dropping a pin can make our destination much easier to find.

A few years later I was in another big city in China, and I was looking for my meeting spot. You might think that my Mandarin speaking ability had improved by this point, but you would be giving me way too much credit for picking up the language. When I walked to the meeting location it was clear I needed more specific instructions. I used WeChat to send a message to a Chinese friend, and two seconds later I received a "pin drop" of his exact location. I opened the pin and walked directly to the very spot where he was waiting. The path was given to me, and all I had to do was follow it. Any time you are lost, a "pin drop" is a welcomed lifesaver.

In leadership, there will be times you feel like you're lost in Beijing. Somehow, someway, you got off track and need to find your way back to your leadership path. The reason for being 'lost' may be no fault of your own, or maybe it is totally your fault. Regardless, how you handle those moments when you are lost in leadership will reveal much about your character as a person and as a leader. Getting lost in leadership is not a matter of if, but when. It will happen, but it is great when you have people to go to who can assist by dropping a rescue pin.

Stepping into the leadership role comes with obvious responsibilities. Leaders are expected to act calm under pressure, have answers in a time of need, provide assurance in times of turbulence, and to have the magical ability to steer the ship to the correct destination in all types of weather. If leaders are honest, there will be those times when we project the aura of calm, give the seemingly right answer, and do it all with confidence when, in truth, we may be full of insecurity as if we are stepping out onto the ledge. Projecting confidence and having confidence often feel worlds apart. How we handle ourselves when lost in leadership will be defining moments in our leadership.

> **BE A DIRECTION MINDED LEADER**
>
> **A LEADER IS ONE WHO KNOWS THE WAY, GOES THE WAY, AND SHOWS THE WAY.**
>
> JOHN C. MAXWELL

The AA, BB, CC & DD's When Lost in Leadership

1. **AA—Admit and Accept.** Being lost in leadership may not be your fault, and it may be the result of unforeseen and unwanted circumstances. How it happened may be important for future learning, but finding your way home is essential for your survival and growth in leadership. When we are lost, we need to admit we are lost and accept help from others. Those you lead will likely be more impressed by the way you accept and admit responsibility for being lost as opposed to you denying and deflecting all blame or responsibility. When you are lost swallow your pride, admit to yourself and to others that you are lost, and be ready and open to accept a "pin drop."

   I experienced this as a new teacher many years ago. I had no real experience handling student problems that came up. However, when I was not afraid to ask for help, I had some great, experienced mentor teachers who were more than willing to drop me a pin. They rescued me, but I had to first admit that I was lost and I had to be willing to accept their help.

2. **BB—BIG BREATH.** When the stress level is high, it is physiologically beneficial to our body to engage in focused and controlled breathing. Controlled breathing sends fresh, oxygenated blood throughout the body which produces a helpful calm over the body and mind. Some participate in Yoga, meditation, Tai Chi or any number of mind and breathing control exercises with beneficial results. When you feel lost in leadership, or when you need to make decisions in times of great stress, take some intentional time to control your breathing and mind. Slow, deep breaths keep you from talking, and sometimes not saying anything right away is a great idea. Find a quiet space, and take a big breath.

3. **CC—CALM and CLARITY.** I love reading about military leaders. In the midst of a raging battle strong leaders somehow remain calm so that they can think with clarity while instructing those they lead. When lost in leadership, one's blood pressure rises. Stress and worry escalate. . Physiologically, our body and brain are negatively impacted. Research shows that under stress the prefrontal cortex will *"shut down, allowing the amygdala, a locus for regulating emotional activity, to take over, inducing mental paralysis and panic."* In this mental paralysis and panic our ability to think clearly and make rational decisions will be affected. To counteract this, find a quiet and uninterrupted space where you can focus with the intent of finding calm and clarity in the moment. Those you lead need you to be, and expect you to be, the force of calm. Like the military commander in battle, if the leader projects calm on the outside, then those whom they lead will often mimic their response.

4. **DD—DESTINATION AND DIRECTION.** There is always pressure on the leader to have a clear destination and direction in mind. Leaders should cast a clear vision and lay out the directional steps they will take to lead the company or group to that destination. Direction provides a clear road map to the target destination.

Sometimes we get lost in leadership. When this happens, Admit and Accept, take a Big Breath, find Calm and Clarity, and, with the help of others, articulate Destination and Direction. The leadership road is rarely easy, but following these principles will help us navigate the road with success.

In my live teacher training funshops, I constantly remind teachers that they are leaders. Leaders will project onto those they lead. If the teacher is stressed it will show, and the students will feel the stress. The followers adopt what the leader projects. I spend a lot of time training teachers in China. It is blatantly clear that teachers and students are under great stress in China. They are under great pressure to be academically excellent. This reality is especially revealed as we explore together this topic of getting lost in leadership. Here is the cycle of pressure: each school wants to be the highest performing school in the city or province. To accomplish this goal, each headmaster must demand the utmost commitment from the teachers to make sure the students understand the importance of this goal. The teachers absorb their leader's stress and, as a result, they often prioritize professional responsibilities to the detriment of their own personal well-being, all of which gets projected onto the students. The students internalize the demands of the teacher, and their parents reinforce these demands with high expectations for future success and for the sake of family pride. The students have little say in their own educational pursuits. Everyone in authority over the student is feeling the stress and pressure to be the best, and this same stress and pressure simply cascades down to the student. It is real, and it is palpable.

The purpose of my teacher training workshops is to shift the focus of relief onto the students. Teachers set out with the primary goal to

> **SHARPEN YOUR LEADERSHIP SKILL**
>
> **WHICH OF THESE THREE AREAS WILL YOU COMMIT TO WORKING ON?**
>
> **VOICE? EAR? HEART?**

prepare students for life. We have deemed certain academic knowledge as necessary so we scaffold learning to build a strong knowledge base that will give students the greatest opportunity for success. But with the stressful demands for performance, I find the student outcomes are less about the acquisition of learning for life and more about the academic performance to elevate the school, the headmaster, the teacher and maybe the student. It is a cycle that leaves the true impact of school on the outside looking in. I try to shift the focus back to the student and equip the teacher with the empathy to "drop a pin" for those they lead.

Whether you lead students or lead others, these three things are done with the mouth, ears, and heart.

1. **Be the voice of reason**—sadly, one does not always receive genuine empathy and emotion from parents, spouses, and colleagues. The voice of reason says you are good enough already, and I care about how you feel more than I care about your performance.

2. **Be the ears of empathy**—many adults (even teachers!) do a poor job of listening because they do too much talking. We have two ears and one mouth, so listen twice as much as you

speak so you can better hear what they feel. In hearing you can communicate empathy which demonstrates understanding.

3. **Show the heart of compassion**. Humans need to feel love. It is one of the instinctive needs we all have. Many leaders, parents, and teachers mean well but forget how to show compassion. I remind all leaders, including teachers to be an example of the heart of compassion because you may be the only source of compassion for someone.

Becoming lost in leadership is not a matter of "if," but "when." It is inevitable. It may or may not be any fault of your own, but as a leader, you bear the responsibility for accessing the resources for finding your way back. The definitive character you will display will be evident in how you handle the times when you are lost. When you feel lost, remember your ABCs (AA, BB, CC, and DD) as a resource to find your way back. And all the while, be the voice of reason, the ears of empathy, and the heart of compassion.

Knowledge is simply good advice waiting to be given, but worthless if you keep it to yourself.

Chapter 9:   EMBRACE THE CONFLICT

At first mention, most people think conflict divides, so they work hard to avoid it. However, great leaders find ways to use conflict to unite and even see it as something to embrace.

I was born the youngest of five children. I admit that, at times, growing up in my home must have been pure chaos. Five children and only seven years separating the oldest from the youngest sounds like a recipe for very little sleep for parents. They had to deal with a large dose of chaos, conflict, and confusion. My parents were great, loving, hard-working, but they were also understandably overwhelmed with the five of us. Talk to any parent today, and they will tell you that one child is a lot of work. Clearly, five children should be reserved only for the superhero parents.

> **FINDING VALUE IN CONFLICT**
>
> **TO AVOID DEALING WITH CONFLICT IS LIKE ROBBING YOUR SOUL AT A CHANCE FOR PEACE**
>
> UNKNOWN

Being the youngest, I may have gotten away with considerably more than my older siblings did. I am not saying I was better behaved than by siblings—although I am sure I was. When it came to parenting the youngest, it is likely that my parents were just so worn down by raising my older siblings that I was able to fly under the radar for most things. As good as that sounds, everyone knows the youngest is the low hanging fruit and the easiest target to pick on. Often viewed as helpless and vulnerable, the youngest is least likely to get in trouble and most likely to fall under the parental veil of protection. In some respects, the youngest may even be seen as untouchable.

The five of us were like a brood of hens where the pecking order was being tested daily. The bigger, stronger, and more aggressive chickens bully their way to the top by pecking the others into submission with their pointy beaks. As the youngest in the flock, I may have been the target of sibling pranks. I recall the time my sisters found my mom's lipstick and decided to transform my adorable baby face into that of a carnival clown. There was also the time when an object in the house was broke during horseplay. My siblings were quick to point the blame on me because they were sure that mom and dad would not discipline little baby Steven. I was also the victim of my siblings pranking at the family dinner table. We were "encouraged" to eat all of our vegetables, but when mom and dad would look away or leave the table, my plate would quickly become the depositing ground for everyone else's lima beans or peas! Now, don't get me wrong. These pranks left no trauma or scars and I have not spent a dime in therapy as a result. Still, all of these harmless interactions provided opportunity for disagreements and resolution, and, in turn, valuable experiences in how to manage conflict.

Over the course of my nearly thirty years working in camps and education I have witnessed and negotiated countless conflicts between children. Sometimes it was like a never ending "he said, she said" dialogue between two or more students—usually who were very good friends—who just got on each other's nerves for some small and insignificant reason. Usually, within four minutes they were running off, holding hands, with the entire conflict in their rearview mirror. Other times, the conflict was much more serious and demanded more facilitation skill to resolve. Each leader must learn conflict resolution skills. Conflict is both inevitable and investable.

Interpersonal conflicts and disagreements often involve lies disguised as 'half-truths' or 'white-lies,' but many of these are easily exposed as bold-faced lies and deceit. There are many times when one individual is just so intentionally mean that the cause of the conflict really does point back to their hurtful intent. Those situations may at first seem unlikely, but as the facilitator, dealing with any conflict requires skill, patience, and a keen ability to listen with cautious care. There are times when the main fault lies with only one individual. The saying, "it always takes two" is not always accurate in interpersonal conflict. Thankfully, these scenarios are not the majority of cases.

As a teacher leader, and as a leader in the camp setting, I have facilitated and negotiated many conflict resolution sessions. I have learned to embrace these moments as an opportunity for my own growth, but more importantly, as an opportunity for the growth of the individuals involved. If the conflict is between staff members, then I must take the same approach as I do with campers and embrace these moments as an opportunity for growth that will lead to greater unity. This is entirely possible as long as I invest the necessary time and attention to the resolution. My philosophy starts with the understanding that conflict is inevitable and investable. How we handle conflict as parents, teachers, camp leaders, or business leaders will reflect on our character and judgment as a leader.

I have been blessed to be able to visit China many times. My love for the culture, people, and the food has been enhanced with each opportunity to travel and absorb what I learn on these trips. Although I have picked up the ability to understand and speak a few words in Mandarin, the ability to read, write and understand the Chinese characters is well beyond my ability. I can appreciate the beauty of the characters used because one character implies explicit meaning. A good example of this is the two unique Chinese characters that are used to represent the idea of conflict. One of the characters used implies danger whereas the other implies opportunity.

As leaders deal with conflict, do we see it as a danger or an opportunity?

Conflict is inevitable, so we must become skilled in how we handle it. Finding resolution is always worth our investment of time, energy, and resources because it leads to personal growth opportunities for all parties involved. Navigating through the conflict will challenge your leadership skills, so buckle up for the bumpy ride.

CONFLICT- DANGER OR OPPORTUNITY?

DO YOU VIEW CONFLICT AS AN OPPORTUNITY FOR GROWTH OR A DANGER TO AVOID?

I do want to point out that the focus of this chapter is when the leader is facilitating resolution between team members and not when they themselves are in the middle of the conflict. That too is inevitable and investable, and so a resolution plan should also be in place when the conflict occurs between the leader and another team member. The purpose of this chapter is with the leader in the role of conflict resolution facilitator.

FOUR "EASY" THINGS TO REMEMBER WHEN DEALING WITH CONFLICT

1. **EMPATHY.** Empathy is such an important concept and something the world needs more of. By definition, empathy is the capacity to understand or feel what another person is experiencing from within their frame of reference. It does not indicate one must surrender their own feelings to adopt the feelings of another. Rather, it is simply understanding where the other person is coming from within their frame of reference. Sadly, the pervasive culture is that if one person vents their frustration, disapproval, or disagreement, those who disapprove are more likely to show hostility than empathy. It seems as if two people can no longer agree to disagree and walk away with mutual respect and understanding. Feelings get hurt way too easily and suddenly friendships are broken over the inability to have empathy. Individuals who are in conflict want to be heard. They believe their reaction is both justified and right and the facilitator must listen with an empathetic ear to understand the complexities. If the facilitator cannot show empathy, then they will not be able to help the conflicting parties see the value of having empathy for each other. A facilitator must be able to show empathy and resolve the conflict with empathy for all.

2. **EARS.** Empathy starts with careful listening. As I have said earlier, we have been given two ears and one mouth, so we must listen twice as much as we speak. Any conflict resolution session must have a clear understanding between all parties regarding the importance of listening to one another. This needs to be modeled first by the facilitator. Allowing all parties to respectfully speak their truth according to their frame of reference will ensure that all are given the opportunity to be heard. Fair and free expression invites opportunity to understand or respect individual positions. Too many leaders talk too much and listen too little.

3. **EXCHANGE**. To exchange is to swap. It means if you give something then something is given in return. It symbolizes a relationship which includes reciprocity. One of the most helpful conditions to establish in a conflict resolution facilitation session is a protocol for how the exchange process is going to work. I typically start the session by acknowledging the circumstances, as I know them, that have led to the need for the session, clearly stating the goal of the session, and setting the ground rules for all interaction. By addressing what happened and seeking to understand why it happened, people can learn how to handle such things that may occur in the future. My typical ground rules provide each person with an opportunity to speak without interruption. We also stress the use of "I" terms such as I feel, I thought, I saw. With the protocol clear, I then facilitate the session making sure the ground rules are honored. People want to be heard, and establishing the concept of an exchange allows all parties to be heard.

4. **EMBRACE**. This may be the hardest but also the most rewarding aspect in a resolution session. To embrace is to hug. When we embrace something, we pull it close to our bodies and close to our heart. The embrace brings comfort. Our goal in the resolution session is to restore the relationship whenever possible. However, there will be times where one of the parties refuses to embrace. This will interfere with the primary goal. In these situations, as a facilitator, we do our best to at least bring an acknowledgement of the full scope of how it happened, why it happened, and how all parties chose to respond. There may or may not be culpability or judgment offered by the facilitator, but presenting a clear reflection of the actual actions is also very important. Someone may leave the resolution table upset and still not feeling "justified," but we cannot control how each member feels at the end of the session. We are trying to avoid misunderstanding,

misperception, and misinformation in understanding the exchange that occurred.

> **CONFLICT REFLECTION**
>
> **THINK OF A TIME WHEN YOU EXPERIENCED CONFLICT. CAN YOU LOOK BACK ON THAT EXPERIENCE AND SEE IT AS GROWTH OPPORTUNITY?**

As a leader, do you see conflict as something you embrace or avoid? Is conflict a danger or an opportunity?

I do not know anyone who enjoys conflict. Most people dislike it because of how it makes them feel. Typically, there is a victim mentality and an aggressor mentality. Facilitators need to handle the situation carefully, understanding the strong feelings that are invested in the situation. The worst thing a "facilitator" can do is to rush to judgment and demand of one party, "say your sorry and don't do that again!" That is not an "investing" response, nor will it yield any personal growth for those involved. The way you navigate a conflict can not only restore relationships but also advance each party's confidence in your ability as a leader. Conflict between team members, students, campers, or friends WILL HAPPEN. It is inevitable. Being skilled as a resolution facilitator means that conflict is an opportunity for growth and not a danger to avoid. Leaders who embrace the conflict as an opportunity will grow, and the people you serve as a conflict facilitator will also grow as you employ these four easy principles of Empathy, Ears, Exchange, and Embrace.

Knowledge is simply good advice waiting to be given, but worthless if you keep it to yourself.

Chapter 10:   COMPETITIVE GREATNESS

I grew up loving all things related to sports. When I wasn't playing sports, my eyes were fixed on the television watching them at the professional or college level. I remember watching Hank Aaron hit his 715th home run in baseball to surpass the great Babe Ruth as the all-time home run king. It was a great sports moment to watch on television. As a boy, one of my favorite weekly shows was ABC's *Wide World of Sports.* For nearly 37 years this show was a Saturday afternoon sports icon. As the show opened, the image of a snow-capped mountain ushered in the announcer saying, "Spanning the globe to bring you the constant variety of sports." But the most memorable line was, "the thrill of victory and the agony of defeat." The hour-long show would feature a variety of amazing sports successes and achievements along with the most miserable of failures and defeats. As I mentioned in an earlier chapter, we do not remember days, but we do remember moments. Moments of success or defeat can surely be memorable. *Wide World of Sports* was a well-mastered show highlighting the greatest and not so greatest, but memorable, sports moments from around the world. I looked forward to it each and every Saturday.

Whereas that show inspired me to play sports, my involvement in sports inspired me and has provided me with the greatest training ground for my love of leadership. Sports can teach so many lessons: how to manage time; how to handle pressure; how to accept instruction, criticism, and praise while at the same time being held accountable. Sports shape an athlete's understanding of the concept of team as well as the balance between striving for self while also being part of a team. Sports teach self-discipline and self-sacrifice, and athletes can easily see the impact of their hard work and training played out in competition against others. These valuable lessons have been used in so many situations in my life. Sometimes the team I was on was the clear favorite to win, but other times we were the "underdogs" and we were expected to lose. One of my favorite sports stories involves the team who was considered the underdog but ended up defeating the giant.

Every four years the world competes in the winter or summer Olympics. There was a time, at least for the United States, when Olympic athletes were amateurs rather than paid professionals. Back then, young athletes would train for many years for a chance to seize one opportunity to shine on the world stage of competition. In these great moments in sports history, gold-medal winners become heroes and legends for their accomplishments. Consider these greats: Bruce Jenner—1976 Decathlon champion to Wheaties' cereal box cover celebrity; Mark Spitz, the mustache-clad, amazing swimmer who won a record-breaking seven gold medals; The unforgettable 1984 gold medal gymnast—the mighty but tiny, 4'8" Mary Lou Retton. As an amateur athlete, winning an Olympic competition would change their economic destiny and national notoriety. Their gold winning performance would usher in countless endorsements and income for many years to follow. As great as their performances were, many of these athletes were favored to win. The chance of victory was far from reality for the 1980 US Men's Ice Hockey team. That year, the Olympics were held in Lake Placid, New York (USA). Having not hosted the Olympics since 1932, America had a strong buzz of excitement and anticipation for these Olympic games. The Men's Ice Hockey team was comprised of mostly unknown college hockey players. Far from being considered contenders, surprisingly, they moved through the preliminary rounds and made it to the gold medal game against the USSR. The match up was the personification of David versus Goliath. The Soviet team was surely the heavily favored and mighty Goliath, while the US was the young David with five smooth stones and a heart of courage seeking to take down the giant. I watched the win on television, and it has become known as the "miracle on ice." This contest remains one of the greatest moments in

Olympic history. Far surpassing individual player's skill, the competitive will-to-win was among the obvious traits for that team.

Although I stopped playing competitive sports many years ago, I have not lost my competitive desire to win. It doesn't matter what I am doing, I want to win. Ping-pong, checkers, a card game, trivia, bowling—it simply doesn't matter what I am doing. I am a competitive person, and I like to win. I have an innate and fierce competitive spirit, and I view most things as a form of competition either against myself or others. I can't help it. It is who I am. Sports helped grow and feed this intense love and desire for the element of competition. I don't want to just be "good," I want to be "great" at the things that I do. I am in no way trying to indicate that I think I am great—far from it. However, I, and many others like me, find the pursuit of goals and accomplishments as a form of competition. Many times, we are competing against ourselves. Some call this "drive"

> **WHAT IS YOUR COMPETITIVE GREATNESS?**
>
> **TO BE AT YOUR BEST WHEN YOUR BEST IS NEEDED. THE ENJOYMENT OF A DIFFICULT CHALLENGE.**
>
> **JOHN WOODEN**

because it steers our actions and motivations. I am not sure why some have it and others do not, but it is clear some people are more competitive than others.

I do not admire every athlete. To me there is far more to competitive greatness than having the best skill in a sport. I look for athletes who inspire me with how they work, how they live, and how they handle victory and defeat. We can learn a great deal about leadership from our athletic heroes. I know many leaders have the same competitive drive as many athletes do. They work hard to improve their leadership skills to be the best, most effective, hardest working leader they can be. Even though they may be at the peak of their power, they rarely rest and would not even think of flipping on the auto-pilot switch. They continue to tweak and modify what they find works well, and they refuse to settle for complacency. Their drive to win the game of leadership motivates and inspires everything they do. My goal in this chapter is a form of self-evaluation for leaders to check and gauge where your desire for competitive greatness may be.

To win at leadership, you must win two games: the mental game and the personal game. But beware, there are things that can damage your competitive greatness.

1. **WINNING THE MENTAL GAME.** Any athlete or successful leader will tell you that to compete, you must have mental toughness. Those who can master control of the mind can more easily master control over their body and skill development. If we can control the flow of what is being fed into and circulating through our brain, we can direct that flow throughout our body's muscles and drive our desire to perfect our skill. Mental toughness controls the muscle systems of the body. If the body is strong but the mind is weak, the foundation is weak. To be competitively great one must master the mind to build the body.

   Three Things That Damage Your Competitive Greatness

   • **Will you be outskilled or outplayed?** Competition is always a challenge of winning and losing. It is one thing to lose because you are out skilled, but it is a totally different problem to lose because you were outplayed by the competition. My mental game was far stronger than my physical game. When I did compete, I could clearly see those teammates and opponents who outskilled me. Not blind or ignoring the obvious, my competitive edge was rooted in my mental toughness. I could easily be outskilled, but I would work hard to never be outplayed. As a leader- your best skill is that which can be found between your ears. Allowing yourself to be outplayed will quickly damage any chances for competitive greatness.

- **What Do You Do With Negative Voices?** We all battle negative and defeating talk from others, but the voices that come from within ourselves do more damage because they come from within. Build your competitive greatness by learning how to train your brain to deliver positive messages to yourself. If you have ever spoken with someone who uses negative self-talk then you understand my point. They embody Eeyore, the classic Winnie The Pooh character. No matter what is happening, the messages that come out of this donkey's mouth lack confidence and are self-defeating. An abundance of negative messages will erode your potential for competitive greatness.

- **Are You Resilient?** As an athlete, I knew I would not win every contest, but I entered each game expecting to win. Although I hate losing, sports taught me how to lose and deal with setbacks and disappointments. Through victory and defeat, I have learned to be resilient. We only become resilient when our expectations and intentions are set high. When expectations are set low, failure is simply an affirming conclusion. Complacent people do not become more

---

YOUR COMPETITIVE GREATNESS

COMPETITIVE GREATNESS IS NOT AN ISOLATED OBJECTIVE BUT ONE THAT RESTS UPON THE FOUNDATIONAL TRAITS NEEDED TO ACHIEVE.

WHAT ARE YOU WILLING TO DO TO BECOME COMPETITIVELY GREAT?

resilient—they become more mediocre. Being resilient is the ability to bounce back after setback or failure, and resilience is one of the greatest leadership characteristics any leader can develop. Set your expectations and intentions high, and welcome every opportunity presented to you that will make you more resilient. Low expectations and low intentions destroy your potential for competitive greatness.

2. **WINNING THE PERSONAL GAME.** As I mentioned, there is almost nothing that I do that I don't turn into a competition to win. A few years ago, my wife and I did "Painting with a Twist." It is supposed to be a fun and relaxing social time where you gather with others to follow the teaching instructor while everyone individually paints the same image. Maybe the glass of wine (possibly multiple glasses of wine) helped lower the expectation and intention of others, but not for me. In typical fashion, I wanted my painting to be the best. It wasn't—not even close, but nonetheless, it was still "game on" for me. My wife has the art-gene passed along from her father, and her masterpiece was worthy of display whereas mine was quickly discarded into the trash bin. I always try to win because I see it as a personal game that helps drive me.

• **Over-Prepare So You Can Over-Deliver.** Competitive greatness is only birthed when you are willing to put in the necessary work. Athletes who refuse to leave practice until they have taken five hundred free throws or until they have kicked twenty five field goals from the fifty yard line become great because they are making sure they are prepared to deliver when called upon. They over-prepare so that when the game is on the line they simply react to the countless shots, kicks, and hours already invested. These athletes control their emotion in the moment and react to the hard work they have already invested. The moment to deliver has been rehearsed so many times that muscle memory happens and emotion is kept under control. They are simply repeating what they have done so many times before in practice. To build your competitive greatness you must put in the hard work when no one is watching so you can deliver when the "game" is on the line.

- **Expect Victory, Analyze Defeat.** I mentioned earlier that I expect to win everything I do. I also readily confessed that I do not win everything that I do. In fact, maybe I lose more than I win. I find it therapeutic to analyze my defeats. Most of what I might consider to be 'success' in my work or personal life was preceded by moments of great failure and defeat. When we analyze what went wrong and how we can do it better, we are able to improve our preparation and sharpen our competitive edge. This process worked well for me as a husband, a parent, a teacher, a business leader, an athlete, and as a human being. Each area in my life I have experienced great failure, but each failure has led to changes in my life that have led me to great victories. Develop your competitive spirit through careful, deep, and honest review and analysis of failure. Analyzing failure puts victory into proper perspective.

- **Make Your Teammates Better.** Some athletes only care about themselves and their individual accomplishments. I assume all athletes want to win, but is their pure motivation for the benefit and success of the team or solely for their own personal success? Kobe Bryant and Michael Jordan earned amazing individual awards, but never once did they step onto the court alone to compete against the five opposing players. They always had four other teammates with which to battle their opponents. Of course, we can understand that athletes (or leaders) want to perform at their highest level, perform successfully, and enjoy the rewards and accolades that may come to them.

A true leader recognizes the impact of colleagues or teammates who have also contributed to their own achievements and success, and the best are quick to acknowledge the contributions of others. Recognize those who contribute to your success. As you succeed, be sure to share the accolades with those who had something to do with your success. Everyone enjoys recognition—just do not forget to share it with those who helped you along the way. Competitive greatness recognizes those who have contributed to the earned success. When you acknowledge others, they are more likely to be more loyal, and this leads to greater opportunities in the future.

One of the greatest proponents and teachers of competitive greatness is the legendary college basketball coach John Wooden. As the head men's coach for UCLA in the 1960's and 1970's, Wooden helped his team win eleven National Championships, ten of which were consecutive championships. This is a remarkable and still unmatched statistic attributing to his coaching greatness. Wooden was a master teacher—able to train his teams to compete and dominate the highest level of collegiate basketball for more than a decade. Any college coach has a daunting task. College teams are comprised of students between the ages of 18-24. Each year a coach loses some experienced players to graduation while they welcome in a new crop of young players as freshmen. A coach is constantly trying to mesh different ages and abilities together in an attempt to be successful. It is a challenge to build a new team each year, but to build a new team and still win at the highest level of competition every year for ten consecutive years is simply remarkable. His accomplishments are a feat likely to never be duplicated. But, as great of a coach as Wooden

> **CAN THIS BE SAID OF YOUR SUCCESS?**
>
> *"Your level of success will rarely exceed your level of personal development because success is something you attract by the person you become."*
> *(Hal Elrod)*

was, his former players will all say that cared far more about their character development than he did about their basketball skills.

Wooden had very strict rules to his method of teaching:

- If you are late for practice you do not play.

- If you are selfish you do not play.

- If you show disrespect to coaches, teammates, opponents, or officials you do not play.

- If you perform poorly in your academics you do not play.

Regardless of your role or status on the team, these rules applied to everyone in any situation. Wooden knew competitive greatness had to be intentionally instilled into their moral fabric so that their individual skills could effectively blend and make the team great. Wooden preached that as long as the team put in the necessary work and self-discipline to be competitively great, they would stand a good chance to win.

A leader is very much like a coach. A leader must set a clear vision—a standard of expectation for performance. As a team builder, a leader selects players to carry out and represent his or her vision and mission. Like a coach, a leader must provide a game plan; constantly evaluate the progress of the team; and when necessary, shift, dismiss, or add new personalities and skills to the team. When there is success, the leader should share it with the team. When success falls short, the leader must carefully analyze and evaluate the methods that led to the defeat. A coach doesn't cast blame on the players, but willingly absorbs the responsibility and works to find ways to lead the team more effectively.

Coach Wooden spent many years perfecting his training system for young men. Yes, they were there to play basketball, but they were also there to get an education for life. He took seriously the task to train his young players for life. His investment in them was sincere and heartfelt, and every player knew without question Wooden's love for and commitment to them. His pyramid of success (shown above) contained fifteen character attributes that he taught and expected each player to not only learn but to consistently live out. The shape of the pyramid was important because each attribute was reliant on the foundational attributes it was on top of. It was a carefully crafted scaffolding plan for their personal development. Sitting proudly at the top of the success pyramid was COMPETITIVE GREATNESS. Wooden believed that if each player was fully committed to mastering the fifteen character attributes in the pyramid individually and as a team, they would be united in working towards the ultimate pinnacle of success and achieve competitive greatness. He never guaranteed victory because victory was not his primary objective. Wooden worked meticulously to prepare himself and his players to be well skilled in the game of basketball, but he knew skill in combination with personal character attributes would train their mental and personal game to give them the best chance to win at life. They prepared their body, mind, and soul to achieve competitive greatness.

If we teach people the building steps to achieve competitive greatness we stand the best chance of achieving success, and they achieve success in their own personal development as well. This is a win-win scenario! The formula of success rests in each team member's commitment level to personal self discipline. As leaders, are we willing to put in the hard work to ensure our level of personal development is the highest it can be? We cannot *expect* others to reach for this goal we are not willing to do reach for it ourselves. If Wooden did not live out his own principles on a daily basis there is no way his players would have followed him. Leaders must live out the principles that will lead to competitive greatness.

Knowledge is simply good advice waiting to be given, but worthless if you keep it to yourself.

Chapter 11:   BREAKING THE SCRIPT

I grew up in a home with a father who was the pastor of a church. This was not only his job but also his passion. He got paid for his work, but he never counted the hours spent against the money he earned. He was one of the lucky ones who got paid for work he found to be purposeful to others and for which he was passionate. I deeply admired him for that. He was a very devoted and faithful man, and he was exceptionally good at delivering the truths of the Bible to those in his church.

As an adult I can see and appreciate more deeply the ways he fulfilled his calling in life. As a young teenager I had a more difficult time appreciating his work—I had a selfish and self-centered attitude, and sometimes I even felt like my life was viewed by the congregation "under a microscope," so to speak. As "preacher's kids" we were expected to attend church and most of the church functions unless we were on our sickbed. Even then, whoever was claiming to be sick had better be able to show a fever of 101°F or higher to get out of Sunday School or a youth group function. If the church doors were open, we were expected to be there. Attending church was basically our forced duty, and it also became our routine.

The church-going-routine was especially challenging when I was a young boy because I found church to be boring. Although my dad taught something new each week, it was impossible for me to sit still, be quiet, and listen intently to the sermon. I mean, sitting still and quiet was already hard for me to do in school, but this was a seemingly insurmountable and unreasonable expectation in church! I may have found it boring because the routine of the service became easily predictable with almost no variance or serendipitous surprise. The format seemed to follow a carefully choreographed cadence. Every service would begin with a quick welcome by the pastor who would try to lighten the morning mood by making the audience chuckle or smile. My dad was a very funny guy and great at making people laugh, and after the lighthearted welcome the crowd would always more easily settle in for the 60-minute service. I remember that I often glanced around the auditorium at the start of my father's sermons to see if I could spot new guests. I would observe them smiling or laughing as I thought to myself, *"you're laughing now, but you have no idea that he is going to speak for 45-minutes straight!"* The next predictable order in the routine had him introduce the worship leader who would lead the congregation in three songs before my dad would return to the podium to make some announcements, offer a prayer, and then take the offering. While the ushers passed the offering plates there was usually a special music selection. After a polite thank you from the worship leader, the congregation would all join in one more song. After the song, my dad would resume control in order to offer one more prayer that signaled to all that the sermon was about to begin. He always spoke for an unapologetic 45-minutes. He was "old-school," and he believed that a sermon should be an exegetical study of the Bible. His messages were always filled with solid "meat and potatoes" content. With almost perfect timing, at 11:58a.m., he would say, *"bow your heads with me,"* and he would lead the congregation in yet another prayer. Those were the magical words that would likely stir me from my sleep. As he would return to his seat, the worship leader would rise and lead us in one final song before we all departed in time for Sunday lunch. The routine (yes, this may have been a rut routine) was predictable, and it was this predictability that some found comforting but that I found to be boring.

The word "predict" means that with a high degree of certainty something will occur. It happens with such frequency and consistency that it becomes a reliable and predictable event. Like how I found the order of a church service to be predictable, many of us have routines we create or follow throughout the course of our day. Someone who is "predictable" forms routines from which they rarely stray. A routine becomes so comfortable that when it is interrupted or thrown off, one might feel "off their game." Being off one's game can be unsettling, and it can lead to anxiety. In truth, routines can be quite comforting because we live well within patterns. Many of us disguise or misname our living routine by referring to it as a "schedule." The routine becomes a pattern that provides comfort, and any deviation from the routine can be unsettling.

Would I have been more alert and attentive if the order of church had been different every week? Instead of the predictable order of service events being the same way each week, what if the leaders decided to mix it up to keep it anything but routine? How would it have been received? I call the action of shaking up the routine as "breaking the script." To effectively break the script we intentionally challenge our predictable routines to ensure that we are not falling into the aforementioned "rut routine." Although many find a routine to be comforting, many others find it to be boring!

The word "improvisation" may help us better understand the idea of "breaking the script." An actor on the stage or on the television or movie set is given a script to memorize and deliver before the camera or in front of a live audience. The actor did not write the script, but she is hired to deliver the words as they are written and as the writer intended them to be delivered. When the camera rolls or the curtain rises if the actor begins to make up her own dialogue or insert words that are not originally written into the script, the actor is improvising and going "off script." Breaking from the routine is breaking the script. As leaders, we must challenge ourselves to "break the script" once in a while to ensure we are not settling into a rut routine and therefore becoming predictable and, possibly, boring to those we lead.

I will be honest—I have a few rut routines in my own life. I am very predictable on certain things, and my family laughs at me for some of them! My morning routine is quite predictable. I get up early and have a cup of coffee and a toasted English muffin with jelly while I have my quiet time reading the Bible. It is my comfort routine that I do every day with a high degree of predictability. However, when I am traveling it is not always easy to maintain this routine. I cannot travel with a toaster or a month-long supply of English muffins and my favorite coffee. My first few days of travel are very unsettling to me because my comfort routine is broken. I must make mental adjustments simply because my predictable routine has been dismantled. I realize my personal and predictable morning routine only impacts myself, but as leaders we must carefully analyze our patterns of predictability to make sure they do not affect our ability to lead others. A routine can negatively impact our ability to lead if we simply work as if we are on auto pilot and have stopped investing into being more creative or spontaneous. We often do not even see our destructive routine patterns without deep introspective searching or unless someone points them out to us. We may be blind to our own destructive routines, while those we lead may see them as an albatross around our leadership neck. If we don't turn away from our destructive routines, these can easily have a negative influence on our team.

TAKE A BREAK

SOMETIMES A BREAK FROM YOUR ROUTINE IS THE VERY THING YOU NEED.

UNKNOWN

Many jobs have repetitive tasks. When I was in college I worked in a machine shop. Anyone who knows me knew this was going to be a disaster because of my inability to focus on things I care nothing about. Each morning I reported to work at 7:00 a.m.. The shop manager had arrived at 4:00 a.m. to begin prepping all the machines in the shop with materials that would be processed by the day shift. When I clocked in and reported to my station the machine was prepped and ready for me. Next to the machine there were containers of parts that I was expected to place into position and shape, drill, sand, and smooth so that each one was identical with the exact same specifications. Some days I would shave, shape, or polish over a thousand pieces. Standing in one spot and repeating the same movements was the most painful mental torture I could imagine. I wanted to quit everyday, and to make matters worse I was horrible at my job—not because I could not do the task but because I was not passionate about the task in the first place. I did not see the end value—I didn't care about those stupid little parts that would be placed on some machine I knew nothing about. There is danger in the monotony of repetitive actions. If we are not careful we stop concentrating, and injuries can happen. I have a visible scar on my forearm that proves this point.

Much of my leadership work is with teachers. Many teachers treat their classroom like I treated my summer machine shop job. They enter their classroom, open their book, write on the board, teach a lesson, ask a few questions, and assign homework. Each chore is completed with predictable precision. Day after day the routine is unchanged. Some students may find this style and routine comforting, but those who are like me find it boring and downright painful. Why won't these teachers vary their routine? Adding variety to the classroom activities would communicate that these teachers care about staying fresh with their methods, and the variety is sure to appeal to students who have different learning styles. What made me hate my machine shop job was the predictability. It is this same level of predictability that makes many students dislike school or become bored in school.

How can you break the script so the routine is not sabotaging your leadership?

Two Step Action Plan: Analyze the Script and Break the Script

ANALYZE THE SCRIPT. We need to analyze how we do things to see if we are operating out of any predictable pattern routines.

1. **Are your procedures painfully predictable?** Business leaders believe in effective systems. Systems are put in place to ensure that processes and operational procedures are more efficient, more easily managed, and ultimately make the business more profitable. It is always a worthwhile task to reevaluate procedures and systems even if, in the end, you find that they are operating at maximum efficiency. Get fresh eyes on the processes and systems, , ask for open and honest feedback, or bring in an outside evaluator to [provide a valuable perspective on how your systems work and on how they are received by those who work closely with them.

   For a teacher-leader, the "predictable script" may manifest itself in your classroom management skills, assessment methods, or teaching model. Each student is a unique learner who may share personality similarities with other students but who may also have learning differences and struggles. Is your classroom management effective for all styles of learners? Do your assessment methods reach different learning styles? Are your classroom procedures mindlessly predictable or serendipitously vibrant? There is value in teachers breaking their own script to keep things fresh and impactful to all styles and personalities of learners. Teachers need to carefully analyze their own procedures and teaching methods in order to ensure that they are not painfully predictable to the students sitting under their teaching influence.

2. **Create Timeless Traditions.** I worked with a dear teacher colleague who taught her math class on such a tight and predictable schedule that it was humorous (not to mention effective!). In the two-weeks leading up to the Christmas vacation she engaged students in a project. For this project she equipped each student with a piece of wood, small nails, and colored thread. Students were then instructed to design string art. Clearly, there was learning value to the project, and the project was always a clear student favorite. The project timing

and process were predictable and routine, but because she was able to make it a timeless tradition she prevented it from becoming a painful routine. The project was carried out by only 8th graders, but the 6th and 7th grade students would see and hear the eighth graders hard at work. This helped build their anticipation for the tradition they would experience just before Christmas break when they reached 8th grade themselves. You can avoid the pain of the routine if you can make the routine feel like it is a timeless tradition. A company Christmas party, a Fourth of July celebration, or some other company picnic or gathering can be shaped into a timeless tradition. We may have or do some predictable things, but it doesn't mean they have to be painful.

3. **Boring or Annoying Behaviors.** We probably all have behaviors that drive other people nuts. For some, they speak certain phrases, use consistent hand gestures, or accentuate with certain facial expressions when communicating. Most of us have some characteristic, habit, or tendency that may be annoying or bothersome to others. We may not even realize we are doing them. Test yourself sometime. Set up your phone, and video yourself speaking. Do you notice hand gestures, frequently overused phrases, or facial expressions that are repeated without awareness? These simple things can impact our leadership in negative ways. I have had the painful exercise of watching myself teach on video. I did not realize I had so many useless hand gestures and odd facial expressions that must have annoyed my audience. I have not eliminated them all, but I have worked hard to improve my presentations to make sure that what I do while speaking does not diminish what I am trying to communicate. Leaders do not want their behaviors to be a distraction from the message. All leaders must carefully analyze their mannerisms and presentation skills or seek criticism from others to ensure that these behaviors (boring or not) do not distract from the value of the intended message.

4. **Meaningless Motions.** I had a middle school music teacher who had all sorts of hand motions when he taught. These motions and gestures happened so much that they ended up being a distraction to many students. There was no medical or physiological reason for these motions, I think he just did them more out of habit than conscious thought. As I previously confessed, I too use meaningless motions when I speak. Sometimes I look more like I am directing traffic at a major intersection with my arms rising, moving, and almost flailing in strange directional movements. Now that I have seen what I do when speaking, I am much more conscious of my movements because I do not want my motions to be meaningless and possibly distract from the value of my overall message.

Careful self-analysis of our script can help reveal areas that need breaking. Obviously, we want our message to be effective, but what we unconsciously or consciously do while delivering the message may, in fact, render the message ineffective. Meaningless, careless, or sloppy habits and routines can be injurious to our effectiveness as a leader.

BREAKING THE SCRIPT. Changing patterns of behaviors and routines will take effort and intention. Change is challenging, and many of us do not welcome the necessary change because it disrupts the comfort of our established routines. However, being able to break the script will expand your leadership effectiveness and influence. It is worth the investment in learning how to effectively break the script. Here are a few considerations when trying to get out of your rut routine:

1. **SURPRISE.** Everyone loves surprises. When we are taken by surprise, our energy is elevated and our senses are invigorated. Make the effort to create surprises in the exercise of your leadership. Simple surprises can be easily manufactured for the benefit of others, and these surprises yield strong rewards

for the leader and for those being led. Another idea is to simply mix up the recurring team meeting or add something fun and unique as a surprise in the workplace break room. The surprise would help break the script, and it keeps you fresh.

If you are a teacher, try stopping midway through the lesson to randomly reward the class with some "social interaction time (SIT). Give the class three minutes to stand up, talk, or simply engage with others. Doing this breaks up your routine, and the surprise will likely increase their attention span for the remainder of the lesson.

2. **MASTER THE MOMENT.** In an earlier chapter I talked about how people remember moments rather than days. If a leader can learn how to "master the moment" it will more likely be remembered and be impactful to others. Like anything, mastering the moment requires some intentional effort. Memorable moments can be manufactured, and with practice you will find that you will be able to create simple memorable moments with ease and with much more frequency.

Recognize birthdays, celebrate work anniversaries, recognize exceptional work performance. Seizing moments like these creates memorable moments in your team. You may even need to "step it up a notch" by making the recognition reason a bigger deal by adding more flare and celebration. Mastering the moment expands a leader's influence and impact.

As a teacher-leader, hold an "HONOR'S DAY." Place a piece of candy at each student's desk so when they walk into the room you will see and hear the reaction as they discover the treat. Undoubtedly, they will all ask you what the candy is for. You can announce that it is HONOR'S DAY and that you want to honor each of them for their hard work. It is a small, simple, yet impactful and fun way to break your script. With a little extra attention and intention leaders can master the moment and expand their influence on those they lead.

3. **ELEVATE THE EMOTION.** Humans are triggered by their emotions. No one is numb to emotion. We all know what "feeling good" feels like compared to feeling bad. Leaders who focus on building strong emotional connections with their team and between team members will reap strong emotional rewards. It may come in the form of loyalty, support, trust, or a powerful feeling of satisfaction for the community culture being created. When leaders find ways to elevate the emotional connections through quality stimuli, they can effectively grow their influence. Maybe the leader sends a small hand-written note to recognize effort in the workplace. Maybe a manager stops by an office to say how much she appreciates the effort given toward a task or project. Or, maybe the teacher-leader stands at the door each morning and gives a fist-pump, high-five, or just a big smile to every student as they enter the classroom. Leaders can easily elevate the emotion of others. In doing so, they are effectively breaking the script.

> **BREAKING YOUR SCRIPT**
>
> **WHICH OF YOUR WORK ROUTINES NEED TO BREAK FROM THE SCRIPT?**

4. **RAISE THE REASON.** People tend to become bored when they lose sight of the reason, goal, or objective behind their efforts. Mundane and repetitive movements such as my summer machine shop job caused me to quickly lose sight of the reason and purpose for my work. As a result, I became bored and disconnected. I had no idea what role the parts I was working on even played in the final product. If you are a teacher-leader, how can you keep your students focused on the reason they need to learn the content you are teaching? How

does it fit into their academic future or their future personal or professional life? A leader who can raise the reason and keep the purpose in the target crosshairs will be intentional and creative in making sure the reason remains in clear focus. Leaders cast a vision, but those whom they lead need to also know how that vision impacts them and what they do.

Leaders who break the script will enter into many win-win leadership scenarios. Those whom they lead will win because they feel valued, recognized, and emotionally connected. They will likely remain alert and on guard because the leader is able to keep the routine from becoming boring. The leader (and/or leadership team) will also win because breaking the script begins to create a culture of unpredictability that is more fun than the routine. Not every script-breaking attempt will be memorable or impactful. This would be an unreasonable expectation. However, even the attempts that flop will be appreciated for the effort, and they will provide valuable perspective for the leader.

When leaders break the script, their actions become louder than words. The demonstrated actions say, "I value my leadership relationship with those I lead, and I am willing to invest my time, energy, and resources to avoid being predictable so that I may maximize my leadership opportunity to influence others in this way." As you make "breaking the script" a passion to pursue, you will guarantee your routine is not a poison to your leadership. Leaders should not just create a team to handle this. I encourage every leader to be part of the process. It is a vital investment in building your company, class, or school culture that will continue to pay dividends long into the future. Making this sincere effort will keep things fresh for you and for those you lead. It will keep you connected with others, and your influence will expand with each intentional effort or serendipitous response. Breaking the script will increase your leadership influence.

Knowledge is simply good advice waiting to be given, but worthless if you keep it to yourself

Chapter 12:   ENERGY

Energy—it's something we all need yet often take for granted. Each flip of the light switch comes with a high degree of faith and certainty that the power flow has been opened and the power we need is instantly accessible. With energy we light up our room or connect our devices which, in turn, connect us to the world. With energy we have a power source that can feed our brains and bodies. We need energy, and we consume it in ever-increasing and massive quantities. We also continually seek new sources for it to ensure long term sustainability. Energy dominates our everyday existence, but it is so easily overlooked until there is a power interruption. When that happens our comforts are suddenly and drastically at risk.

Traveling through China or America it is common to see multiple energy producing sources. Many of these sources are easily visible to the naked eye such as nuclear, solar, wind, or hydro energy-harnessing stations. In wind belt areas, the landscape is decorated with massive wind turbines that spin in the breeze and generate electricity from naturally occurring wind. China has the largest hydro-electric dam in the world—the Three Gorges Dam in Hubei Province. This dam produces 22,500 megawatts of electricity each year. For perspective, one megawatt can roughly provide electricity to 1,000 homes! Whether it be coal, gas, oil, or other energy harnessing sources, we recognize the value of energy as a life-essential service and requirement to live comfortably. Most of us do not appreciate or know how it is produced, stored, or delivered. We only care that we have it when we want it, and to some extent, we also care how much it will cost us to keep it. How energy is harnessed, stored, and delivered may be easy to comprehend for those who work in the energy business, but to the average citizen consumer the science behind the process is often a mystery. However, when we are "out of energy," we suddenly realize how crippling it can be to our comfort and survival. Preserving energy to light up the world is crucial. In like manner, Every leader must generate and preserve a "leadership energy" in order to be an effective leader.

I can recall the worst flu I ever had. In fact, my wife and I got this flu at the same exact time. Our energy was totally sapped out of our body, and we required the goodness and assistance from family to feed us and take our kids to and from school. It was three days of sickness that we will never forget. Prior to that sickness, and ever since then, my energy level, like electricity, is something I took for granted. Once you don't have it, you crave for its restoration and suddenly take great interest in respecting the power supply. The moment I am sick, or the instant my lights don't work, I become immediately interested and grateful for what turns out to be just another fleeting moment of appreciation.

I recently watched a good movie called *The Boy Who Harnessed the Wind*. It was about a farming family in Africa who was significantly impacted by a drought. The entire family worked frantically to grow and sell crops to sustain the family and feed those who also relied on their crop yield. As the reality and impact of the drought carried on longer and longer, the scenario grew more and more dangerous. As the young 12-year-old Malawian boy named William watched his family struggle, he shared with his father his idea for how to harness the wind in order to pump water from below the ground surface to provide life-saving hydration for the dying crops. William had thought long and hard about this idea, and in his curious and creative mind he felt it would work. Excited with the idea, William needed to find and assemble various pieces to build out his idea. His father had no faith in the wild dreams of his young 12-year-old son. Persistent and undeterred, William refused to give up. Taking his father's bike (the value equivalent of a car to this poor African family) he chopped it up to harvest the parts needed to build his windmill project. Recognizing the desperate and dire situation, the father finally agreed to support the ingenuity and curiosity of his son. Using an old car battery and wire retrieved from a junkyard, the boy built a windmill that successfully pumped water and saved the crops, the family business, and the lives of others. They were elated to see the water pumped from the ground—sourced by harnessing the natural flow of the wind. The life-saving flow of energy was NOT taken for granted, but practically worshiped. The boy's curiosity for how to harness the wind to create the needed energy was born out of necessity to have it.

Energy is precious! Many of us try to conserve it, but many can also be seen wasting it. Because we do not make it, it becomes an easy thing to take for granted. We use it with little consideration of how it is harnessed or sourced. But when energy is gone, and we fall sick or

> **CAREFULLY GUARD YOUR ENERGY SPACE**
>
> **ENERGY IS CONTAGIOUS, POSITIVE AND NEGATIVE ALIKE. I WILL FOREVER BE MINDFUL OF WHAT AND WHO I AM ALLOWING INTO MY SPACE.**
>
> **ALEX ELLE**

must deal with a drought or loss of power we suddenly feel lost and in the dark because we don't have the energy we need. The boy who harnessed the wind did not take it for granted. His family's desperate need for energy motivated the boy to pursue a new source with intense passion because he knew it was essential to their literal survival. Leadership energy is often taken for granted. Energy in leadership is vital. The source and sustainability are precious, and the health and survival of our leadership depends on the free and steady flow of it.

Do you know a "high-energy" person? You know, the type of person who is always moving, producing, or doing something that propels them and others forward? Their activity level is like that of the Energizer Bunny® who just keeps going and going and going. They always seem full to the brim with energy and vitality, and they are rarely ever seen as depleted or lacking energy to do more. Of course, we likely also know the direct opposite—the individual who has low energy output and appears to be one small step away from being a zombie. Their production is low. Their capacity to do more is as low as their faintly beating pulse. Just having them around seems to suck the life-energy out of the room. Your energy level is something that will either attract or repel potential followers or even other leaders.

Individuals are unique and so is their internal energy level—whether it is innate or manufactured. The expectation is that leaders should have a steady flow of energy because it somehow makes them charismatic or enigmatic. Followers seem to love high energy output from their leaders. People expect leaders to be "movers and shakers," and followers expect a leader's energy levels to always be visibly high. Whereas some leaders are energy producers, others are categorized as energy consumers. Leaders who are energy consumers have low output, and their pulse is lower. They are more likely to put a room to sleep with their low energy than to wake it up. Managing or leading others requires us to be proficient at understanding the source of each person's energy.

The esteemed author and renowned leadership coach, Bruce D Schneider, teaches leaders to value the resource of their leadership energy while stressing the importance of helping others to harness their energy to achieve success. Schneider helps leaders evaluate their source and level of energy so that they see it as a valued and protected resource that is necessary for them to be truly effective leaders. I would like to reshare his seven levels of Energy in Leadership, but I recommend buying and diving into his book *Energy Leadership: Transforming Your Workplace and Your Life From The Core*. (2007)

Understanding the Energy Leadership Index (ELI). ELI is a self-assessment tool designed to measure one's personal energy level. Using data from personal responses to specific scenarios, this assessment tool assigns a numerical value based on the type of energy applied to the given situation. The goal is to better understand how we might harness energy and thus better determine and apply positive energy in our life and workplace. Understanding personal energy levels will contribute positively to a better understanding and balance in all areas of life: work, relationships, spiritual connections, and personal health. Energy is not just some output of personality or pizzazz. Energy can be mental, spiritual, emotional, and physical. With each level of ELI Schneider provides "core emotions" most often connected to the energy level. When you take the ELI assessment tool do not expect to fall nicely into only one level. Most often we are a blended mix of ELI levels.

Level 1

These leaders are <u>critically self-aware</u> but often fail to act. Level 1 leaders typically have <u>low self-esteem,</u> work in crisis mode, and lack productivity. These leaders don't have a real plan for where they are going personally or professionally, and they typically spend their energy reacting to circumstances as they are presented. Their communication skills are poor to nonexistent, as is their ability to truly inspire and motivate others. <u>Low energy output, high energy consumer.</u>

Core emotions: guilt, self-doubt, hopelessness, fear, worry, depression

Level 2

For these leaders, <u>actions and results come from a place of anger and defiance</u>. The focus is on others, stress, disappointment, resistance, struggle, control, and entitlement.

Oftentimes, interactions with these types of leaders feel like a zero-sum game in which their world consists of winners (them) and losers (everyone else). It is common for Level 2 leaders to be micromanagers. Whereas they tend to see themselves as high energy producers they are primarily consumers who also sap the energy out of others.

Core emotions: anger, resentment, hatred, blame, greed, discord, pride

Level 3

A Level 3 leader thinks positively, and their emotions come from a place of forgiveness. Actions and results may include rationalization, justification, tolerance, and coping. Many leaders rest in this level because levels 1 and 2 are focused on negative traits that most people do not see in themselves. Level 3 leaders consider themselves as having moderate energy output and moderate energy consumption. They tend to be the peaceful leader who avoids conflict, and, in doing so, he or she avoids giving clear guidance and direction.

Core emotions: relief, peace of mind

Level 4

Level 4 leaders' focus is on their team. <u>They genuinely care about others, and they don't take anything personally. Instead, they maintain an objective view or circumstances and people. They tend to be playful, generous, supporting, helpful, and self-caring</u>.

This kind of leader typically performs best in human resources, customer service and sales because of their exceptional people skills.

<u>My observations: I see many teachers in this level.</u> Their leadership is built on compassion for others (students) and energy output is strong and consistent. Love and compassion drive their energy.

Core emotions: compassion, love, gratitude

Level 5

Level 5 leaders are typically <u>lively and extroverted leaders who love to live life</u> to the fullest and don't let the past get in the way. They are open-minded and focus on the organization rather than just themselves. Often, a level 5 leader will <u>see challenges as opportunity for greater growth and development.</u> These individuals don't try to change others who are different from them. Instead, they focus on accepting and reconciling differences. Energy output is high, and many people rally around this type of leader. They are well liked and equally well respected.

Core emotions: peace

Level 6

These leaders are driven by their <u>intuition, and they are often creative geniuses and strong visionary leaders.</u> Individuals at this level of leadership see others around them as an extension of themselves, which fosters an attitude of empowerment and achievement among team members. Level 6 leaders love it when everyone wins. These leaders are often considered brilliant and conscious leaders. They attract a lot of followers because their energy input and output are so high. My observations: Many teachers start here only to have the many aspects of their job sap their energy and reduce their level of energy to a lower-than-desired level that is not natural and where they do not want to be.

Core emotions: joy

Level 7

The 7th and highest leadership level is often the hardest to achieve, and few people have ever experienced it. It is characterized by a complete lack of blame, shaming, and fear of failure.

Level 7 leaders don't make judgments and, unlike Level 2 leaders, feel that winning and losing are illusions. They are fearless, and they create well, but they also observe.

Core emotions: passion

Maybe this level is achievable but also difficult to sustain. Maximum Energy producers who consume only what they need to sustain. These gifted leaders possess exceptional leadership skills marked by genuine humility and gratitude.

Now What? Time for an Energy Inventory

Ascending to a higher leadership energy level requires your deep and honest introspective inventory. Without energy output leaders don't grow, and not growing inhibits one's leadership influence, or worse—lack of growth may even suffocate it altogether. A leader cannot be an effective leader and remain an energy consumer. Strong leaders maintain their energy independence and constantly take personal inventory to stay connected.

If you feel you cannot dig deep enough to understand your leadership strengths, look for a trusted and valued mentor leader who would be willing to help you with this personal inventory assessment. It should be someone who you respect as a leader and not simply a best friend who will only tell you how great you are no matter what they honestly think, see, or feel. Do not be afraid to turn over all of the rocks because you want to reveal things both seen and unseen. Leaders are not perfect, and we build leadership habits based on experiences lived.

Give attention to those positive and negative habit-forming experiences so your inventory assessment is thorough, complete, and, most of all, helpful.

I wrote in an earlier chapter about the things in life that are unwanted, unplanned, and unappreciated. When these kinds of things happen, if your energy status is that of a consumer, these events are likely to have a greater [negative] impact on you than if you are an energy producer. A skilled leader who is an energy producer will face these moments head on because they know that doing so is the only path to move forward and produce growth. Energy producers recognize that managing the peaks and valleys in leadership and in life comes from deep within, and success in navigating these difficult times is directly proportional to their personal energy output. Our energy independence is manufactured internally, released under control, and carefully protected as a resource needed for sustainability. Let your passion be the recipient of your energy output. Let your purpose be filled by the energy from leading others with intention and integrity as it will be meaningful to self and others. Leadership is influence, and when you become energy independent you too will have learned how to harness the wind.

WILL YOU HARNESS THE WIND?

WHAT CAN YOU DO TO IMPROVE YOUR ENERGY LEVEL?

Knowledge is simply good advice waiting to be given, but worthless if you keep it to yourself.

CONCLUSION

Conscience, Character, Courage

I recently listened to one of my favorite podcasters, Mike Rowe. If you don't know him, check out his television show *Dirty Jobs*. You will likely recognize his face if not his rich baritone voice which has been helping to make many Discovery Channel shows memorable. He is delightful, witty, and whimsical. He is for sure a guy I would love to sit down and share a cup of coffee with. His Podcast, *The Way I Heard It*, episode #238 *He Has Nodded on Our Undertakings* was an interview with Westminster Theological Seminary President and

> **TAKING THE FIRST STEPS**
>
> *A JOURNEY OF A THOUSAND MILES STARTS BENEATH ONE'S FEET.*
>
> ANCIENT CHINESE PROVERB

Professor of Historical Theology, Dr. Peter Lillback. Dr. Lillback spent the better part of thirty years researching historical documents, letters, and diaries to write *George Washington's Sacred Fire,* a book on the leadership contribution of America's first leader, President George Washington. I encourage you to check out this episode and let me know if you were as impressed as I was. (Seriously—email me your thoughts: Advantage-USA@comcast.net)

The key to great leadership can be boiled down to understanding three very important "C" words: Conscience, Character, and Courage. A leader must possess all three of these attributes. Conscience is the inner feeling or voice that serves as a guide for the rightness or wrongness of one's behavior. The moral compass of a leader is clearly observed in the actions of the leader. Watch what a leader does, and you will know the inner moral compass called conscience that directs that leader. The actions reveal the character. You cannot separate one's conscience from his or her character. The umbilical cord that connects them is the heart and soul of a leader's deepest guiding light. Courage is simply the perseverance of action to live true to oneself by acting in a way that fulfills the conscience and character of the leader. A leader who lies, cheats, or cannot admit mistakes cannot claim to be a leader who values truth, honor, and humility. Sad, but true, leaders are fallible humans. Mistakes are painful, and sometimes mistakes are devastating although, thankfully, we can often rebound from our mistakes and press forward. Guard your leadership reputation carefully. The leader is what the leader does.

I am the sum of the many leaders who have invested and poured into me throughout my life journey. I have been influenced by my parents, my siblings, my wife, my children, teachers, coaches, employers, managers, friends, and countless others who have all added colorful strokes of paint onto my life leadership canvas. Their bright and beautiful strokes were painted both intentionally and unintentionally—transforming me into the leader I am becoming. The picture being painted may not always be clear or evident to myself or others, but please be patient because I know it is a painting that is still in progress. I thank you all, and I thank God that He is not finished with me yet.

If you have the opportunity to influence anyone then you are a leader. Embrace the role of leader, but know there is responsibility that comes along with this role. I have set out to convince teachers that they are leaders who happen to also teach. Too many teachers see themselves as data givers, and because the assessment and performance demands are so great they forget to recognize their role as leader. A teacher is the CEO of his or her own corporation within each class. How you lead, teach, instruct, inspire, and challenge each person who follows you comes with great responsibility. Those whom you lead are looking to you for more than just dates, names, equations, and formulas. They want someone to inspire them to reach yet to be determined potential and possibilities.

Keep your CEO job description simple—influence others. Obviously, we all have the potential to influence others both negatively and positively. Step up and prepare so that you can ensure that the influence you leave is a positive one. Their life depends on it.

I have chosen to share these lessons in leadership because *knowledge is simply good advice waiting to be given, but worthless if you keep it to yourself.*

Our ability to lead and influence others creates a legacy that can extend far beyond what any of us can imagine. I have had the blessing to tell the influential teacher-leader in my life how he influenced me in a profound way. Because he selflessly poured into me, the entire trajectory of my life was changed. God used him and others in profoundly powerful ways to paint onto my life canvas, and I deeply appreciate his investment in me. Maybe my friends, children,

> **WHO HAS CONTRIBUTED TO YOUR LIFE CANVAS OF**

grandchildren, or even strangers will read this and reflect on individual lessons in leadership taught to them by their own heroes. Consider those who have contributed to painting on your life's canvas. And remember, you are still a work progress, but you are on your way to becoming a masterpiece.

ABOUT THE AUTHOR

First and foremost, I am happy to be a husband, father, and grandfather to those I love deeply. I have been married to Ruth, my college sweetheart for more than thirty years, and she has been my champion and cheerleader. She is also the mother to our five children: Tara, Shannon, Mackenzie, Steven, and Erin. Currently, we have 4 beautiful grandchildren, but we selfishly want more!

I am driven to do work that is purposeful to me and meaningful to others. This has kept me in the fields of education and summer camps for more than thirty years. To support this passion of working with children and families, I have invested time and energy into a myriad of other ventures.

Advantage-USA

One of my ventures has been in the area of international educational consulting. As the President and CEO of ADVANTAGE-USA, I work with international students to help them find the "right fit" school for their international studies. I also do speaking engagements and conduct teacher training workshops (funshops) to help train teachers on how to create a more connected classroom experience with, and between, their students.

www.Advantage-USA.org Email: Advantage-USA@comcast.net

Back in the early 1990s, needing to survive on earning a private school salary, I began designing summer camp experiences for children. I eventually started my own business, CAMP CONCEPTS, INC. under

which I now administer several summer day camp experiences for children ages 2-16.

www.CampConcepts.org   Email: CampConcepts@comcast.net

In 2019, I launched IMMERSIVE EDUCATION ASSOCIATES, INC. (IEA) with two partners. IEA provides guidance to schools seeking to embrace Virtual, Augmented, and Mixed Reality education technology and resources to enhance learning. VR, AR, and MR provides high student and teacher engagement, improves learning retention, and will soon usher in the next revolution in disruptive educational experiences.

www.ImmersiveEducationAssociates.com

Email: ImmersiveEducationAssociates@gmail.com

In 2021, I accepted the role as Chief Operations Officer of GLOBAL CONNECTIONS FOUNDATION. This NGO has a mission to better connect Kenya to the United States. We seek to empower others towards greater self-reliance through education and entrepreneurial initiatives that will transform lives, destinies, and create opportunities for peace, harmony, and prosperity.

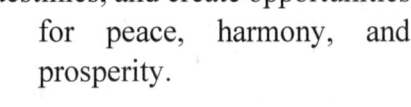

www.GlobalConnectionsFoundation.com
www.gcfkenya.org
Email: Shaines@gcfkenya.org

Please consider giving of your time, talents, and money that will bless yourself and others in the process.

My Other Book

Check out my other book, *The Art of Facilitation: Discovery of the Group Growth Process* ©2020. This is a book written for leaders who seek to sharpen their group facilitation skills. This book was also written with teachers in mind, but the principles within its pages are practical for anyone who is in a leadership role. The book is written in both English and Mandarin—dual translation all under one cover.

Paperback ISBN: 978-1-7348772-0-5
eBook ISBN: 978-1-7348772-1-2

OTHER WAYS TO CONNECT

 Steve Haines

Thank you for reading. My goal is to honor God by doing the things which I am passionate about and that I find meaningful to me and purposeful to others. As long as I keep this as my goal, I will never have to work a day in my life.
Steve

ENDNOTES

Introduction:

Dweck, Carol S. <u>Mindset: The New Psychology of Success</u>. New York: Random House, 2006.

Chapter 1:

https://www.workersresort.com/en/design/pixar/

Chapter 2:

https://www.businessinsider.com/thomas-edison-in-the-obstacle-is-the-way-2014-5

https://www.business2community.com/strategy/the-great-value-of-disaster-0160198

https://www.livescience.com/63645-optical-illusion-young-old-woman.html

Chapter 3:

https://www.sasktoday.ca/south/in-the-community/do-you-want-the-truth-or-a-good-story-4108591#

http://www.andrewnewberg.com/books/words-can-change-your-brain-12-conversation-strategies-to-build-trust-resolve-conflict-and-increase-intimacy

https://www.everydayhealth.com/columns/therese-borchard-sanity-break/420/#:~.

*https://brm.institute/neuroscience-behind-words/ The Neuroscience Behind Our Words

Posted August 8th, 2019 | Category: BRM Capability, Business Relationship Management Research, Professional Development | Contributed by Lindsey Horton

**English Standard Version of the Bible. The ESV® Bible (The Holy Bible, English Standard Version®) copyright © 2001 by Crossway Bibles, a publishing ministry of Good News Publishers. The ESV® text has been reproduced in cooperation with and by permission of Good News Publishers. Unauthorized reproduction of this publication is prohibited. All rights reserved.

The ESV® Bible (The Holy Bible, English Standard Version®) is adapted from the Revised Standard Version of the Bible, copyright Division of Christian Education of the National Council of the Churches of Christ in the U.S.A. All rights reserved.

Chapter 4:

Life Jar illustration adapted from https://medium.com/illumination/the-jar-of-life-d36bf673dc90

Covey, S. R. (2004). The 7 Habits of Highly Effective People: Powerful Lessons in Personal Change (25th anniversary edition). New York: Simon & Schuster.

Chapter 5:

https://www.campaignlive.com/article/hard-things-easy-easy-things-hard/1498154

https://www.jackcanfield.com/blog/how-to-find-your-purpose-in-life/

Shortform summary of "The 7 Habits of Highly Effective People" by Stephen Covey.

Chapter 6:

Purchase The Power of Moments book, https://heathbrothers.com/the-power-of-moments/

Chapter 7:

https://www.widewalls.ch/magazine/most-expensive-van-gogh-paintings-auction

https://www.investopedia.com/financial-edge/1010/top-6-reasons-new-businesses-fail

Elrod, Hal. The Miracle Morning: The 6 Habits That Will Transform Your Life Before 8:00AM 2012. John Murray Press, London, England.

https://www.brainyquote.com/quotes/michael_jordan_127660

Chapter 8:

https://www.ncbi.nlm.nih.gov/pmc/articles/PMC4774859

Chapter 9:

https://ardencoaching.com/your-brain-on-change/

Chapter 10:

https://www.youtube.com/watch?v=Vv368yWOSas

www.TheJohnWoodenCourse.com

Elrod, Hal. The Miracle Morning: The 6 Habits That Will Transform Your Life Before 8:00AM   2012. John Murray Press, London, England.

Chapter 11:

https://knowledge.wharton.upenn.edu/article/breaking-the-script-how-companies-can-make-themselves-memorable/

http://www.dadcraft.com/break-the-script/

https://austinmoms.com/2019/08/25/in-a-rut-break-the-script-through-the-power-of-defining-moments/

Chapter 12:

https://www.energyleadership.com/book

Conclusion

https://podcasts.apple.com/us/podcast/the-way-i-heard-it-with-mike-rowe/id1087110764

Now take your life canvas that has been painted on by many leaders along the way and go write your lessons in leadership.

www.ingramcontent.com/pod-product-compliance
Lightning Source LLC
Chambersburg PA
CBHW071247070526
44583CB00017B/2368